Getting Started in Genealogy
or, How To Leave a Legacy
and Have Fun Doing So

Getting Started in Genealogy
or, How To Leave a Legacy and Have Fun Doing So

Charles Rice Bourland, Jr.

iUniverse, Inc.
New York   Bloomington

iUniverse books may be ordered through booksellers or by contacting:

iUniverse
1663 Liberty Drive
Bloomington, IN 47403
www.iuniverse.com
1-800-Authors (1-800-288-4677)

Charles R. Bourland, Jr.
4 Hasleiters Retreat,
Suite 104
Savannah GA 31411
www.genealogyhowto.com

Because of the dynamic nature of the Internet, any Web addresses or links contained in this book may have changed since publication and may no longer be valid. The views expressed in this work are solely those of the author and do not necessarily reflect the views of the publisher, and the publisher hereby disclaims any responsibility for them.

ISBN 978-1-4401-5438-6 (sc)
ISBN: 978-1-4401-5437-9 (ebook)

Printed in the United States of America

iUniverse rev. date: 07/27/09

Foreword

Charles Bourland has written the consummate "How to" book for the amateur genealogist. I have known the author for a dozen years and it was his encouragement that gave me the incentive five years ago to delve into genealogy and learn who my ancestors were. At that time I knew nothing beyond my immediate grandparents and next to nothing about them. Without the author's initial guidance and instruction I never would have been able to make the progress I have made.

I only wish that this book had been available when I started. Its sound advice would have saved many hours of effort and provided a much more orderly approach to my search. From the first emphasis on a Work Plan, which is vital, to the presentation of web sites useful to the beginning genealogist, the author captures the essential elements necessary for a successful ancestor search. One who has not undertaken such a search can not anticipate the amount of paper and data that will be generated. Consequently, this book stresses the absolute necessity to have a filing system and to maintain trip reports to keep things in reasonable and working order. Our author offers a relatively simple, but effective plan for the collection of source material. In essence this book will help the amateur genealogist avoid the pitfalls of poorly organized searching and constructively speed the credible discovery of information.

I am very proud of this book and the help it will bring to amateur genealogists and also proud to be called friend by Charles Bourland. All those who are eager amateur searchers, Charlie, will find themselves very much in your debt.

Richard G. Osborne
Barnstable, MA.

June 28, 2009

Table of Contents

Table of Contents, continued

Preface

I started researching my family in 1995 without benefit of a how-to book, course or other help. I got some advice along the way, usually from someone also researching, but the help came as the need arose and as a consequence led to delays, missed opportunities and so forth.

Several years ago I began teaching a 12-hour course entitled *Getting Started in Genealogy* at the Armstrong Atlantic State University (AASU) in Savannah, Georgia under the Lifelong Learning Institute aegis. I have also taught the course at the Skidaway Community Institute and The Marshes of Skidaway Island. Every class has included a few personal friends who in social situations would cajole or jeer at any missteps one takes and I have survived the worst they have offered.

This book introduces the generally important necessities of beginning the journey into researching your family and leaving a legacy. It offers a touchstone for nearly all the aspects one faces in genealogy. For example, it includes identifying and citing Sources, preservation of documents and artifacts, writing a book and publishing it, and many other areas.

I believe **if you will follow the Work Plan, step by step,** you will find an exhilarating and exciting hobby, and will perform a rewarding and valuable service for your descendants. You will find it is work, but fun as well. Serendipities await you at every corner.

Within the book I reference various software choices, web sites and other copyrighted and trademarked items. The owners are cited in Appendix 1.

I am indebted to my wife, Susana Bourland, my son, Barry, and my friend Carolyn Zalesne for their editing skills and support as well as all of my students whose blank looks helped me identify that which was being badly explained and caused changes both to the course and eventually this book.

- Charlie Bourland

Chapter One

INTRODUCTION

Many of us grow up with fanciful ideas of our past, some planted by relatives who think they descend from someone famous or our own conjectures that our name is the same as another in the news or book we are reading and perhaps we are related.

In my case I either conjured up the thought, or else my mother placed it in my mind, that we descended through her family from the William White who came to America on the *Mayflower*. I have learned that nothing could be further from the truth as her family landed in Maryland and not Massachusetts.

But beyond this rather minor conjecture I was not interested in genealogy until I had retired from business. In fact, getting the young interested in genealogy is almost impossible. I was not interested until I took a car trip from St. Louis, where I lived at the time, to Tampa to visit my oldest son. I suggested we drive through Mississippi and then Alabama and the Gulf coast as I had never been there. Also my favorite author at the time was Willie Morris, who was born in and had placed many of his books in Yazoo City, Mississippi. When we got to Yazoo City, I remembered an old family story that my much admired Uncle Henry, a World War II hero, had unveiled a statue of Jefferson Davis in Vicksburg. So I proposed we go and see that statue and its plaque. Uncle Henry apparently had unveiled the statue because he was the then youngest son of a Civil War veteran, my maternal Grandfather, who fought for the South.

When we arrived at the Vicksburg Memorial Park I went to the front desk and told a Park Ranger I wished to see the Jefferson Davis statue. I told him the story of my uncle. He looked at me doubtfully and excused himself for a few minutes.

He returned with a pamphlet that had been produced under the direction of my grandfather and included pictures of he, my grandmother with the title of Secretary and my then 8 year-old Uncle Henry.

My wife exclaimed, "Charlie, he's wearing blue! He fought for the North." I had thought the South.

Wow, far from home in a place I had never before set foot on I find a piece of my family's past and it changes many notions of them and their life and what I think I know of that life.

It turned out that my grandfather had been selected by the Governor to have constructed and installed a Civil War Memorial for West Virginia as all States in the war had done. In so doing he had enlisted his family as support staff. And he had fought on the side of the Union.

All of this started a series of questions in my mind: what else that I thought was factual could actually not be true, who was I and from whom did I descend? What had shaped our family and its traits? These reflections started me on the exhilarating and exciting hobby of Genealogy.

After spending countless hours researching and publishing some eight books on my ancestors, and then teaching the subject in my local State University at the Lifelong Learning Institute as well as other locations, here is how I believe one should "Get Started in Genealogy." And by the way, you will see what a major mistake it was not to get interested at an earlier age when I spent many nights within a stone's throw of my past with no inkling of that past.

Here is how the course which I teach, and this book, starts!

My Personal Background

Let me say right off, this book is not about me, truly; but since I am not a genealogist who works for others except in teaching a class and writing this book, and my personal experiences and examples are all I have, I must use them to illustrate points about genealogy which are important.

First let's set an objective for our studies. The French writer Emile Zola (1840-1902) said: "*To have a child, to plant a tree, to write a book – that is a full life.*" It may seem now like a large, unattainable objective but my job is to prove over the next pages how easy it is to write a book. As to the why, it seems to me you are thinking about genealogy in answer to the question, "where did I come from?" Certainly you should leave something behind for children or grandchildren as you answer that question. Leave what behind? Well, a book would be nice.

With that objective, let's start our studies toward the publication of a book, or books, about our heritage. At least, let's get started on an exciting hobby.

So, what already do you know about me?

Correct, my father carries the same name of Charles Rice. But in addition, there may be a Rice somewhere in the past.

Okay, what is important here is that I was born and raised in the coal fields of West Virginia. I lived in five towns with populations of less than 500, and then moved to a town of 2,000. I never left the state except to visit grandparents in western Kentucky a few times until I was 14. Then I added rural Virginia to my list of homes. In other words, I consider my background as small town provincial and I never thought I had a past outside of the states of West Virginia, Kentucky and maybe Virginia.

I will also disclose that I lived, as an adult, in the Hartford, Connecticut area for

35 years and drove to Boston and its environs at least 1,000 times over the years without ever knowing this was where many of my ancestors came in the 1600s.

I will likewise tell you I now know I do descend from a *Mayflower* family, but it is my father's and not my mother's.

You will uncover a little later why I have 56,000 people in my database but am related to less than 20,000 of them.

Books Written

- The White Family of West Virginia
- The Ancestors of Elizabeth Ann Bobbitt
- The Ancestors of Mary Elizabeth Cardwel
- The Bourlands: Tracing a Family
- The Bourlands and Allied Families From Massachusetts and Delaware
- The Bakers: Tracing a Family

I don't mention the list of my books to trumpet my writing skills or productivity, but (1) to provide some of my important surnames with the hope those in the class (or reading this) will have the same names, and (2) to make the very valuable point that researching the distaff names is not only important but opens many valuable avenues for significant research. Most of your relatives do not have your surname.

Tracing the women in our background is not as easy as the men since women generally changed their names to that of the husband, and the older women tended to be more reticent and create less paperwork and paper trails than the men.

But to continue with my books.

I believe strongly in capturing a wide swath of people around my parents and relatives. This includes neighbors, pallbearers, those who buy or sell us property, those named as executors of a family will or as inventory takers and others. This does not mean to place all these names in your database, but on a list somewhere so that when the name surfaces a second or third time, it might begin to make sense to see what you can learn about that family.

Why? This will become clear later but generally in the 1850s and before marriages occurred between neighbors, sons-in-law became executors and so forth. If you fail to capture their names, tracing a grandparent can become much more difficult.

Back to the books. It turned out with the 56,000 names I had some considerable data about more than 100 families from Hopkins County, KY, the birthplace of my father. So I created chapters of a book on these families and sent it to the Hopkins County Genealogical Society, from whom I had received over the years much useful assistance.

Let me add that my Bourland family came to Hopkins County in 1807 and remained there for 170 years. Relatives live there still. For some readers, such geographic longevity may not exist; your families may have moved on westward after but a few months or years and thus you will not have one advantage as did I in collecting certain useful information.

Books - continued

- Miscellaneous Hopkins County Families
- Bourland Personal
  - Father's Autobiography
  - My Autobiography
  - Coal camps
  - Extensive family interviews
  - Trip reports
  - Vacation Diaries
  - Some special memories of my sons

Finally I created a Personal Book (PB). All the other books have been put into the major genealogical libraries and family members have received a copy. This Personal Book was strictly for my descendants.

That book includes my father's autobiography as well as mine. I believe it is nearly criminal for both parents to fail to write an autobiography. Our children have no direct experience with the first, let's say, 30 years of our life and miss much of the last 30 and they will want to know. Not now perhaps, but when they are in their 60s, 70s and 80s they will wish they knew. And think of your great-grandchildren!

Here is an example. During World War I my father was stationed in Koblenz, Germany and was billeted with a German family. His autobiography did not provide the address or the name of the family. When I by chance drove through Koblenz years later, imagine my disappointment in not being able to visit that home, perhaps chatting with a person who "remembers that American" and could relate a story I never heard.

The Personal Book (PB) includes a monograph on coal camps. I lived in several of them for 22 years. My children have never seen one. My monograph may help them visualize more of my upbringing. You in turn will have some experiences your children are not able to share because the world continues to change and the past becomes lost unless a history is created.

Next in the PB are some rather personal interviews of close relatives and write-ups of trips I took to collect genealogical information. More on this later.

Then there are diaries of major vacations taken with notes on what we did, saw, ate and where we stayed as well as reflections on the country or places.

Finally, in the PB there are some highly subjective thoughts on my children and their lives over time.

Now here are some comments on the 56,000 names. The number is certainly excessive, but here is the reason. I started out merely wanting to know more about the family. A few years later I changed my Objective. The new Objective was to write a biography or perhaps a novel about my father, whom I admired a great deal. However, much of his early background was lost so I began collecting data on anyone in his town about his age, living near him and so forth. I thought that with that information I could probably construct a reasonable novel with parts that were true.

Later on, after finding the wife of a GG Grandfather and learning her descendants came into Massachusetts early, I found that many avenues opened up for research. I again changed my Objective to one of multiple books and no novel.

Okay, with that self-introduction out of the way (but remember, there are many lessons therein) let's talk about a Work Plan to make you into a Book Writing Genealogist. Or if you prefer a less ambitious title, just a Genealogist.

Chapter Two

A WORK PLAN

In order to meet a specific objective – to write a book, or if you prefer, become a genealogist – we all need a Work Plan.

I urge you to execute this Work Plan step by step unless geography prevents you. By geography I mean when I suggest you visit your birth town and certain libraries in other locations, it may be inconvenient to do so because you will need to travel. That problem is understandable. My experience with those who skip around otherwise in the Work Plan indicates they usually fail to make meaningful progress. So, as best you can, go step by step.

Right here at the starting block, I will tell you that I strongly believe that a computer and specific genealogical software are the best tools for the job. They are not required, but surely make life easier!

Work Plan:
Buy a Computer and Genealogy Software

- For the PC
  - Family Treemaker
  - Rootsmagic
  - Personal Ancestral File (PAF)
  - Master Genealogist
  - Legacy
- For Macintosh
  - Reunion
  - Personal Ancestral File (PAF)

For the computer, my personal choice is the Macintosh as I believe it is much safer from viruses, easier and more intuitive to use. Plus, I have one.

The PC is already in many homes, so let's make no further issue of which computer. Just that having one will make genealogy easier and enlarge resource opportunities. But know that many perform genealogy the time-honored way, with paper and pencil.

As for genealogical software, you can use Google to find it and then you can evaluate the listed choices. There is one advantage to Family Treemaker in that it already exists in many homes and is owned by Ancestry.com. Thus, you can to good effect use the on-line version of that software and receive many benefits from Ancestry. com. Then you can download your findings to your own software and computer. There are additional comments on Ancestry.com later.

Personal Ancestral File (PAF) will run on both the PC and the Macintosh and has been free in the past. (Many things change over time and what I write here may by the time you read it be changed by the owner.) The other software choices will cost between $35-$100.

Reunion and Legacy had in the past common producers and both can be considered excellent choices.

Next you need to buy legal sized folders and a box of computer labels. Legal folders are required because you will want to save many Source documents and many of these are on 11 x 17 paper, including such items as court documents, wills, marriage licenses and the like.

The labels will be used to number your Source documents with a unique number so that they may be retrieved easily and quickly. Sequentially number your labels and then place one on each Source document you find. Record the fact in either a spreadsheet or your software, which process will be discussed in greater detail later.

Then you will need a copy of *The Handybook for Genealogists*, published by the Everton Publishers.

This invaluable book provides a map of each state and its counties, a history of each state and its counties, an address and telephone number for each county and whether they have birth certificates, death, divorce records, probate records and the like. Additionally, how each county was created over time is given. Further, Everton includes migration paths, trails and the like. You will find yourself using this book often and silently thanking Everton for its availability.

The book provides the history of a county because you will find a family living in X County in year 1, Y County in year 2 and Z County in year 3. In fact, they may never have moved, but the name of the county changed.

While I do not consider the following book a requirement, it is nonetheless most useful in describing the various groups that immigrated to America in the 1600 and 1700s. It provides a useful historical perspective for your work.

Albion's Seed: Four British Folkways in America. This cultural history explains the European settlement of the United States as voluntary migrations from four English cultural centers. Families of zealous, literate Puritan yeomen and artisans from urbanized East Anglia established a religious community in Massachusetts (1629-40); royalist cavaliers headed by Sir William Berkeley and young, male indentured servants from the south and west of England built a highly stratified agrarian way of life in Virginia (1640-70); egalitarian Quakers of modest social standing from the North Midlands resettled in the Delaware Valley and promoted a social pluralism (1675-1715); and, in by far the largest migration (1717-75), poor borderland families of English, Scots, and Irish fled a violent environment to seek a better life in a similarly uncertain American back-country. These four cultures, reflected in regional patterns of language, architecture, literacy, dress, sport, social structure, religious beliefs, and familial ways, persisted in the American settlements.

Albion's Seed - Four British Folkways in America
by David H. Fischer, 1989

- **1629-1640 Puritans**
  - Eastern GB into Massachusetts
  - Middle class
- **1640-1675 Royalists & Indentured Servants**
  - Royalists and Indentured Servants into Virginia
  - 75% servants, mostly younger sons
- **1675-1725 Friends and Quakers**
  - Into Delaware
- **1717-1775 Others**
  - Northern borderlands & Ireland into back country of America
  - Not for holy reasons but worldly gain

It is necessary to say – USE YOUR COMPUTER AND GENEALOGY SOFTWARE! I find many people buy it and then worry about many things and forget they have the software. Or they avoid facing a sometimes difficult learning period. You can and should always call the vendor when you face a problem and nearly all of them have responsive Help Desk people. So call them if you experience problems.

Thus the next thing you should do is to get to know that software by using it. At a minimum you know facts of birth dates, locations and the like for yourself, your family and your parents, maybe even your sibling families. Enter that data and get used to how you enter data and how you can retrieve reports. Learn how to enter Source data into that software.

Most software systems are similar in that the initial screen focuses on the husband and the wife, reflects what is known about each as to birth and death dates, and shown above them are their parents. Below them are shown the children of the couple. Between the parents and the children are data on the marriage.

Shortly you will be familiar with that software and have placed known data on your immediate family into it. It is time to see what the world knows and can share about your family.

Since Ancestry.com is a for fee web site, it is important that you perform well the previous tasks of the Work Plan. You should first make sure you are ready to put into your software the data that you have in your own possession and are comfortable with both the computer and the software, including use of the Internet. When that is completed and you have time to devote to the Internet, you should join Ancestry.com.

Work Plan -continued

- Subscribe to Ancestry.com

- Subscribe to the New England Historical and Genealogical Society (NEHGS)

If you are from or your family is from New England, you will find the New England Historical and Genealogical Society (NEHGS) of extreme importance, (**www.newenglandancestors.com**). They are the oldest in the country and an extraordinarily useful organization and web site. More on this later. Likewise, look at **www.CyndisList.com** so you are aware of its value when you are ready to broaden your search.

As you continue working, work from the "known" to the "unknown." This means if your name is Smith and there is a famous General Smith born in 1713, do not start with him to get to you. Start with you and go to him, or, go wherever your research takes you because most often you will find General Smith (1713) is not related to you at all. I took the "fact" that my mother was descended from William White of the Mayflower and spent over two years determining that she, and hence I, were not related to him. Subsequent research proved my father was William White's descendant, but look at all the time I wasted by going from Unknown to Known. So, start with you and work back to your ancestors. And by the way, my parents were not cousins.

Work Plan - continued

- Work "known" to "unknown"
- Use a wide focus
- Document your sources
- Organize your data
- Visit sites
  - Cities, counties
  - Libraries, Historical and Genealogical Societies

I have already talked about using a wide focus. That means keep track on paper, not in your database, of important names you locate such as godparents, witnesses to a will, takers of inventory for a probate, buyers of items from a probate inventory and so forth. If you see the same name appearing several times in several documents, research that family surname as there will be a good chance somewhere before or after the time period one of that family with marry into yours. You will see later where some ten surname families of mine were contiguous neighbors.

So how do you work from the known ………

First by preparing a questionnaire that seeks specific data from relatives. An example follows in Appendix 4 of an excellent and often used questionnaire called a Family Group Sheet (FGS), or sometimes called a Family Group Record (FGR). Copies are available at familysearch.org and other sites.

The FGS form includes a small writing area for Notes of a biographical nature. The best approach is to write a cover letter or e-mail to each relative that asks that they fill out the form, but with some specific instructions. For example:

- Please include if known the FULL name of each person, including middle name;
- Please include COUNTY in addition to city and state, if known;
- Because I intend to write a book for the use of the extended family, I would ask that you send me an e-mail or other electronic communication addressing biographical items you would like included. You should consider covering your schooling, work career, homemaker career, hobbies, extracurricular activities in the community and the like. If you prefer to merely write this information on the back of the FGS, that is all right as well;
- This data will not be placed on the Internet but remain within the family. I will treat all you submit with confidentiality, beyond the book.

You should review old photographs to remind you of older relatives and to isolate pictures that are appropriate for your book. The reverse of the photographs may well include the name of an otherwise unidentified person and be dated for the event.

And of extreme importance, interview your older relatives before losing them so that you capture the old family oral histories. Those histories may or may not be factual, but they nonetheless are a part of your family's history and may serve as a counterpoint to the truth as you can uncover it. Remember my thinking incorrectly that my mother was a *Mayflower* descendant. Indeed, because my father's grandmother died in childbirth, my father never even knew her name. Consider taping these interviews, transcribing them and saving both. Prepare a list of questions for your interviewee so you are well prepared.

Make sure you talk to your siblings. I can not tell you how many times I have heard of, or experienced, a sibling saying "oh, by the way I found this box up in my attic which came from Mom's attic and it has some stuff you might want." You truly must gently push relatives to look for old items long out of sight.

Soon you should start a Pedigree Chart so that you can measure your progress and remind yourself where you should be going. A sample Pedigree Chart can be found in Appendix 5. One would start by putting himself as #1, his father

Why Do All of This?

- Family reunion
- Famous person
- Health issues, anticipated
- Publish to honor
- Visit to homelands
- Who am I; Where am I from
- Where do 6° of separation take me

as #2 and his mother as #3. Then his grandparents tied to their child on back as far as is known.

Let's stop a minute and ask, "Why are we doing all of this?."

Well, you may find your family has been having reunions. I was 63 years old before realizing my family had been having reunions every year since 1889. Such history books as you may create are a big hit at a family gathering. They can be special hits if you uncover a famous cousin doing well, or even one doing evil, which can be more fun.

Many people do genealogy to uncover health issues that have affected family members historically. Conversely, one may feel especially close to a father or grandfather – or a grandmother – and wish to honor them. Also you may be planning a trip to a foreign country of family origin and wish to take considerable information with you to get closer to the history of the family.

Lastly, I will attempt to prove how determining where 6 degrees of separation takes you is worth your investment of time and effort in genealogy.

Cervantes in Don Quixote says: *"One that brings and derives its original from princes and monarchs, which time has defaced by little and little, 'til at last it ends up in a point like a pyrimide; The other owes its beginning to people of mean degree, and increases gradually to nobility and power; So that the fifference is, the one was once something, but is now nothing; and the other was once nothing but is now something; perhaps therefore, I may be one of the first mentioned division, and my origen, upon inquery, be found high and mighty."* Life of Don Quixote Vol. 1, p119, ed 1770.

In addition to participating in an exhilarating adventure, getting a chance to meet new relatives and having fun, there is what I call **The Wellness Factor.** I must admit I got this concept from a first cousin I had not seen for 50 odd years, and he is a mental health specialist. Here is a letter he wrote me after the first book I published, a hard-bound book with many pictures and biographies of descendants of John Bourland (1762-1843).

1450 Preston Forest Square, Suite 203, Dallas, TX 75230
972-503-4803
www.happyme.com   bourland@happyme.com

Saturday, March 31, 2001

Charlie Bourland
4 Hasleiters Retreat
Savannah, GA 31411

Dear Charlie:

Well, *The Bourlands: Tracing a Family* only gets better with time. I was, once again, reading it this morning. It is becoming one of my favorite books, Charlie. As you might expect, I tend to put a psychotherapeutic twist on things. Along that line, the book you have written is a wellness gift for anyone in the family who reads it. Allow me to explain:

In my practice, I work quite a bit with people who have either lost - or never developed - a strong sense of self. Books like yours, Charlie, give the reader, family member, a sense of belonging - a sense of having roots; therefore, a feeling of significance and importance as a person. And who cannot benefit from more of that?! It occurred to me that you may not be aware of what a mental wellness gift your book will no doubt be for Bourlands for many years to come - especially the youngsters.

Can't you just see little Angelica or Charles R., perhaps when a little older, plop down on the sofa with a new friend, book in hand, and say: "Look, here's a book about my family ... and here I am, on page 97!"

Anyway, I just wanted to share these thoughts with you and, once again, thank you for working so hard to produce this family heirloom.

Warm regards,

Gary N. Bourland, MA, LMFT, LCDC
Clinical Director

Gary of course is exaggerating and overly complimentary, but I do believe his point is well taken.

In the meantime, let's add some levity to illustrate the point that genealogy can be fun.

Some Tombstones

On the grave of Ezekial Aikle in East Dalhousie Cemetery, Nova Scotia:
Here lies
Ezekial Aikle
Age 102
The Good Die Young

In a London, England cemetery:
Here lies Ann Mann,
Who lived an old maid
But died an old Mann.
Dec. 8, 1767

A lawyer's epitaph in England:
Sir John Strange
Here lies an honest lawyer,
And that is Strange.

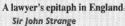

More tombstones

In a Ribbesford, England, cemetery:
The children of Israel wanted bread
And the Lord sent them manna,
Old clerk Wallace wanted a wife,
And the Devil sent him Anna.

Playing with names in a Ruidoso, New Mexico, cemetery:
Here lies
Johnny Yeast
Pardon me
For not rising.

In a Silver City, Nevada, cemetery:
Here lays Butch,
We planted him raw.
He was quick on the trigger,
But slow on the draw.

To insure we are on the right path, let us review the various tasks of the **Work Plan** that have been identified to this point. The Work Plan is an annotated guide to your becoming an efficient and successful genealogist:

- Buy and learn to use a computer, especially on the Internet

- Buy and learn to use genealogy software, especially using your own immediate family data as a learning process

- Buy labels and sequentially pre-number a few

- Buy legal sized manila folders to house Source data

- Buy Everton's *The Handybook for Genealogists*

- Join Ancestry.com, NEHGS and CyndisList

- Work from the known to the unknown; that is, from you and your spouse toward the ancestors of both

- Work with a wide focus on people, that is, those touching your family events in a personal manner

- Prepare transmittal letter or e-mail for, and send, Family Group Sheets (FGS) to relatives; ask for names and addresses of other relatives

- Review old photographs; save as appropriate

- Interview older relatives, perhaps taping them

- Talk to your immediate family on what "may be in the attic"

- Start a Pedigree Chart

We will now continue with the next steps in the Work Plan. The next such review will be found in Chapter 5.

Chapter Three

INTRODUCTION TO THE GENEALOGY INTERNET

To get you into the Internet, let me first send you to

http://wc.rootsweb.ancestry.com

But here's a secret – if you have a relatively recent computer you do not need to type the "http://." Your Browser (Internet Explorer, Firefox, etc.) will do that for you. Sometimes a "www" must come before the "wc", but not often. So this time just go to wc.rootsweb.ancestry.com. This is, as of this writing, a free Ancestry.com offering. Here is what you will see, excluding advertisements. Perform actions which are hand-circled and/or have arrows.

WorldConnect Project — Connecting the World One GEDCOM at Time

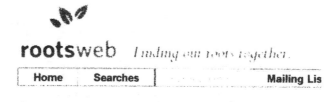

FAMILY HISTORY BOOKS

"I am 100% delighted! I look forward to creating ordering many more books in the future."
— Bill Cerrett, Sandbach, England

**Search Family Trees
at WorldConnect**

Advanced Search

More than **480 million** names on file

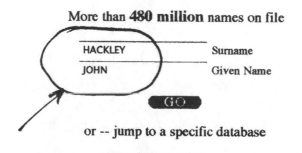

HACKLEY	Surname
JOHN	Given Name

GO

or -- jump to a specific database

The example above is one of my ancestors, John Hackley. You should put in one from your ancestry. Keep in mind that most individuals and certainly most web sites do not permit living people to be put on line except described as "Living Person", to protect privacy rights. So you must go back a bit in time for your name or else use mine for this exercise.

When you enter "Hackley, John", here's what comes up, again minus the ads, and at the bottom of the page:

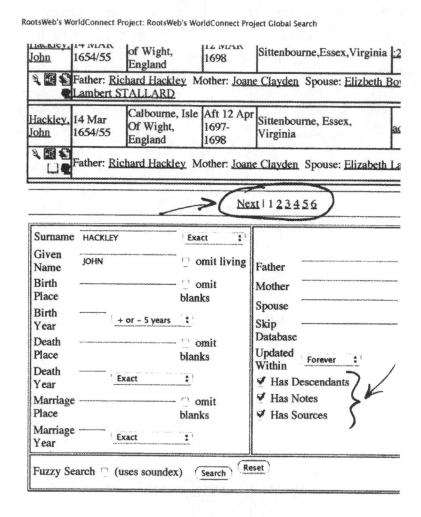

What comes up are the first several John Hackleys in the "worldconnect" database of Ancestry.com. I say first several because you can see there are 6 or more pages of such data on John Hackleys – remember there may be, over centuries, many John Hackleys. If you know his birth or death date or close to it, you can insert that data for the next search to get closer to your man.

You will also notice there are certain icons under John's name and you want as many icons as possible because they signify Parents, Children, Notes and Sources, etc. So use a check mark before the "Has _____" to center in on the very best data available, probably. I say probably because this is your task, to locate the best data possible before proceeding.

Once again you will click on Search and the next page comes up:

rootsweb *Finding our roots together.*

| Home | Searches | | Mailing Lists | Message Boar |

Best-seller for a re

With source templates, book b
Family Tree Maker 2009 just g

Arthur B Clark

Entries: 4912   **Updated:** 2006-05-02 08:46:54 U
Contact: Karene Stevens

Index | **Descendancy** | **Register** | **Pedigree** | **Ahnentafel** | **Downloa**

- *ID:* I3489
- *Name:* John HACKLEY
- *Surname:* Hackley
- *Given Name:* John
- *Sex:* M
- *Birth:* 14 Mar 1654/1655 in Calbourne, Isle of Wright, England
- *Christening:* 14 Mar 1655 [1]
- *Burial:* Mar 1698 Sittenborn, Essex, Virginia
- *_UID:* 797BC1062F87F0428F9B84EEEF9F6E2B6667
- *Change Date:* 16 Apr 2005 at 21:57:53

Father: John Richard HACKLEY b: ABT 1627 in New Port, Hampshire, England
Mother: Joane CLAYDEN b: ABT 1623 in Calbourne, Hampshire, England

for
th

There you find considerable data on this particular John Hackley as compiled by a researcher. The data will or can include birth, death dates and locations, wives and children, and sometimes a significant Note on the history of this John Hackley. Many times there are listings of the Sources of the data and perhaps the person or web site which provided it.

And there is one more extremely important piece of information. The name of **another person researching this surname.**

What you see near the top is a Contact person and e-mail address. He or she may be a cousin, but at a minimum s(he) has researched your same surname and may have considerable other data to exchange with you. In my example "Karene" is the person in question, another researcher.

If you have now identified the correct John Hackley, or your equivalent, you must review the other individuals which "worldconnect" provides because often there are additional data that others do not have. You do not want to miss a single fact available from numerous researchers. And each version represents yet another potentially valuable researcher of your ancestors.

So here I will give you a Goal on your path to your Objective of writing a book. The Goal is to get in contact with 2-300 people, we will call them Colleagues, throughout the nation (world) researching your same surnames. "Karene" here, or whoever she is in your case, may or may not be a cousin, but send him/her an e-mail and ask if they would like to "exchange" data with you. The address may be too old, they may no longer be interested, but most times you will come up with an e-mail Colleague who can help directly or at least suggest others who can.

Put these 2-300 people (Colleagues) onto a spreadsheet with columns for name, address, telephone number, e-mail address and "surname(s) researching." Over time they may prove useful.

	1	2	3	4	5	6	7
1		First	Date First				
2	Last Name	Name	Contact	Surname	Surname	E-mail	Telephon
3							
4	Bethel	Rose	4/5/97	Bourland	Gordon		501-782-87
5	Cardwell	Ina	3/20/98	Cardwell		ina@aol.com	409-635-03
6	Chapman	Peggy	8/6/97	Baker	Woodruff		
7	Couchot	Virginia	5/7/06	Davis			
8	Crowe	Ward	7/9/02	Cardwell	Loving		270-821-58
9	Givens	Doug	5/4/02	Bourland		dgivens@bellsouth.net	
10	Laffoon	Jim	6/9/04	Bobbitt		Jlaffoon@aol.com	855-635-87

But also remember, some or all of this data may be incorrect, so treat it accordingly. We will later talk about Source data and proofs considered acceptable.

A MAJOR SOURCE OF USEFUL DATA

We have been to one useful Ancestry.com site earlier called "worldconnect", which was found at **wc.rootsweb.ancestry.com**. Let us go to another site.

This one is **www.rootsweb.com.** Some of the sites on the Internet will require you to join Ancestry.com for a monthly, quarterly or annual fee. The ones seen here next are free as of the writing of this book and are very useful. So, follow the instructions within the slide. What you are finding is that many surnames in the nation have a mailing list which if you subscribe, AND YOU SHOULD, you can read other persons' queries or responses to queries concerning that surname. You can see the old queries any time you wish, but in addition the new ones will come

Work Plan - continued

- Go to *rootsweb.com*
  - On Home page go to *Mailing Lists*, left side, near the bottom
  - Then go to *Index*
  - Now go to *Surnames* and the alphabet of choice
  - *Browse* and *Search* surnames archives (bottom)
  - Read queries, record data and Colleagues
  - Sign up to join your Surname lists
  - Then go to *State* and *County*
  - Last, go on Home Page to *Message Boards* and Surnames

to you automatically. Don't worry, you will not fill up your mailbox, and if you do, you can easily unsubscribe. Make sure you Search and Browse the archives as there you will find useful data from more than 10 years of activity.

A close reading will show astute questions asking where certain data was found (Source), where a certain person fits in the family, maybe an alert that an old tintype or photograph is available on eBay and so forth.

What else is available on these pages?

If you have been paying attention to your reading, here are more Colleagues with their e-mail addresses. Again, they may not work out as helpful, may not even be available anymore with that address, but you need to get 2-300 Colleagues to meet your Goal and here are many to use for that purpose.

Next on rootsweb.com is the County, and queries posted there.

Once again a close reading will suggest there are excellent data available here. Certainly you should follow the instructions and subscribe to receive all new queries. Equally important, you should go to the Archives to look at all the old queries from the last 10 years or so.

Lastly here you should go to the web sites of all counties in which you believe your ancestors lived. This is done by going to

www.rootsweb.ancestry.com/~kyhopkin

where the tilde after the slash is found on the upper left side of the keyboard and the state is abbreviated (here Kentucky as KY) and the County is six (6) characters or less (here <u>Hopkin</u>(s) County, KY).

Many counties have excellent and highly informative data available, as indeed many cities and states do. So never forget that Google is a highly powerful search tool and can turn up addresses you would have a hard time guessing, such as what the Internet address of a particular city or county is.

You may complain there is too much data in the archives. Maybe the following letter will convince you otherwise. The letter is from a person who took my class and whom I had sent a note mentioning there was a book in which he should be interested:

Charlie, Thanks for thinking of me. I have a complete, original edition of the book, and have recently purchased a 2003 reprint of the book and a CD of it. Since class ended, I have reviewed thousands of e-mails on Rootsweb and have picked up a lot of good info. I've made copies of pertinent e-mails that I've come across and am now about to assemble a database in Excel of the information and Sources. When that's completed, I'll start entering my lineage into Master Genealogist.
I'm having fun!   Ken

A surfeit of data is a serendipity and as Ken says, a big help and a lot of fun. And by the way, you should Google all of your family surnames!

Chapter Four

DOCUMENTING YOUR SOURCES

We have covered the first several tasks of our Work Plan and will now discuss documenting the Sources of your data and seeking proof of their accuracy.

Research is more than names, dates, and places. It is a family historian's goal to find the records and documents and then analyze the accuracy and credibility of those Sources. Family-history standards require a higher level of proof than does most litigation. Genealogy accepts no margin of error. A single error in identity will be multiplied with each generation beyond the error.

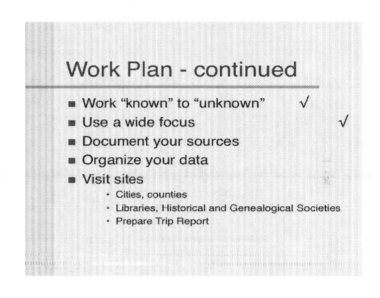

There are two levels of Source document proofs:

- Primary Source – one created by someone with first-hand knowledge or created at or about the time an event occurred. Examples would be a marriage license, death certificate, probate record, or proper copies thereof.

- Secondary Source – everything else.

It is the responsibility of the genealogist to provide a "convincing level of proof" and where questions arise such as "nearly identical data." an articulation of the thought process to support the conclusion must be made.

I will not take these concepts much further here but provide you with what is considered the Bibles: two books by Elizabeth Mills. The first is *Evidence! Citation and Analysis for the Family Historian*, 124 pages.

The second book is *Evidence Explained: Citing History Sources from Artifacts to Cyberspace*, 900 pages.

The Gospel

- "Evidence! Citation and Analysis for the Family Historian", 124 pgs.

- "Evidence Explained: Citing History Sources from Artifacts to Cyberspace", 900 pgs.

Elizabeth S. Mills
Genealogical Publishing Company

As a generalization, I would recommend the second book only to those intending to publish beyond the family, and then only for truly odd Sources beyond the normal.

This leads next to a discussion of Citations, which are the means by which you provide to the reader of your work the reasonableness of the information.

Now we find the reason for the labels and the legal folders you bought.

Let's say the first item you find is your marriage license. Put a label on it, probably in a clear place near the bottom and put the number 0001, because it is the first and we will number your items sequentially. In my case for no good reason I separated my Source documents between paternal and maternal. So my number was actually B001. See the example below.

A	B	C
B001	Application - for Membership, Charles R. BOURLAND, Jr. #62013	for the Children of the American Revolution
B002	Book - "The Bourlands in America", published 1978	Carl and Mary Read, authors.
B003	Newpaper article - on Kopperston, WV, from The Charleston Gazette	of April 20, 1978. Kopperston was built and run by C.
B004	Newspaper article - Know Your Neighbor, C. R. BOURLAND	from the Charleston (W. Va.) Gazette, December 7, 195
B005	Letter - from Herb V. Brown, President Brown Fayro Company	of April 5, 1941 to congratulate C. R. BOURLAND on hi
B006	Newpaper article - H. R. BOURLAND helped write the revised Constitution	for Kentucky in 1890. Article from Madisonville (KY) Me
B007	Letter - From E. B. BOURLAND to C. R. BOURLAND dated	September 11, 1947 concerning family tree and the Pei
B008	Story - This is a story of Dr. Reece BOURLAND capturing the outlaw	Pennington who had killed a man named Davis. It is co
B009	Family tree - of the Bourlands, created by C. R. BOURLAND,	probably just prior to publication of B002, the "Bourlan
B010	Book - "American Government, Not for Teenagers Only",	by Earl H. BOURLAND in 1988; ISBN-0-9609350-2-9, p
B011	Book - Extract, from "History of the University of Michigan";	1906 by B. A. Hinsdale. Page 351 and 352. Article on E
B012	Book - "The Loving Family in America", an extract supplied by	Alene Loving COOK, in a letter dated January 1995; als
B013	Letter - from Roger BOURLAND to Genealogist Read	on his ancestry.
B014	Notice - The Bourland Society, incorporated in Kentucky to	reclaim Old Richland Church Cemetery in Madisonville,
B015	Obituary - Death notice for Charles R. BOURLAND	
B016	Obituary - Death notice Margaret White BOURLAND.	(Missing?)

You will notice the spreadsheet has essentially two columns, one for the sequential number and one for the description. The description starts with an entry from the taxonomy of the items you will find: Books, Marriage Certificates, Obituaries, Probate records and so forth. This permits one to use the "Sort" command in Excel or another spreadsheet software on the B column to bring all the Books or the Obituaries together to more easily locate the one searched for. When you get, and you will, several hundred Sources, it is not easy to remember them all. An easy lookup method becomes important.

Now let me emphasize, the spreadsheet is not needed if you learn how to use the Source capabilities of your genealogical software and if it has a Search command likewise allowing you to bring, let's say, all the Books together in a list. But many of us start entering data before being fully acquainted with our software. If this is you, make sure you enter all spreadsheet data into the genealogy software as soon as you can.

A well written book will require a bibliography. The listing of books as discussed above allows you to create a bibliography easily.

While a Source might well be an e-mail from Mary Smith with an e-mail address, and while NOT a convincing proof of the data, recording this will nonetheless help you avoid the question, "where in the world did I see that," or, "who told me this." If you look at enough Sources from other genealogists, you will soon learn the proper method of their preparation and need to refer to the Elizabeth Mills book only in special situations.

Proof Standard

While I have discussed earlier the need to prove your work by obtaining and providing the Sources for your facts, here I want to add additional thoughts on this important point.

Proof Standard

- Conduct reasonably exhaustive search
- Collect complete, accurate citations
- Analyze and correlate all information
- Resolve all conflicts
- Arrive at a soundly reasoned, coherently written conclusion

The Proof Standard is shown to the right.

Below is an extract from one of my books. While I do not provide you with the referenced "Workpapers," you can certainly determine the proof standard has been applied in this case.

According to White, Scott and Allied Families *by Emma Siggins White, the famous "Breeches Bible" of William White has been preserved. This Bible is an edition of the Genevan version, known as the "Breeches Bible" as it used "breeches" instead of "aprons" in Gen. iii, 7. This Bible was printed in London in 1588, and is filled with records of the White and Brewster families. According to these records the book was owned by William White in England in 1608, and was brought over in the Mayflower. It has a record of the birth of Peregrine White, the first child of English parents born in this country. "Sonne born to Susanna White dec 19, 1620. yt six o'clock morning." There are some childish pictures and scribbling in the book, including a caricature of Peregrine, a sketch of a meeting house, and an Indian drawing his bow. The book was owned in 1895 by S. W. Cowles of Hartford, Connecticut.*

However, subsequent research proved the Bible a fake. S. W. Cowles bought it in 1892 from a Manchester, CT bookseller named Charles M. Taintor (who would be a cousin of William White as well as of this Compiler, see the Taintor chapter) for $12.00. He donated it by his will to a son and it ended up in California with the son's surviving wife. She gave or sold it to a lady in Texas by the name of Miriam Lutcher Stark who in turn donated it to the University of Texas. John B. Thomas, III removed it years later from a book cart, became interested and determined it was a fake. See B737 for the research papers associated with this effort.

Here are some sample Sources:

1. B084, Research papers, from the Shepard Room of the Springfield, Greene Cty, MO Library for Local History and Genealogy. This effort on Charles Rice CARDWELL, including obituary, Alms House logs, and others. Discloses death as 5 May 1927.

2. B050, Marriage Certificate, C. R. CARDWELL and Emily C. GRAHAM on March 15, 1876. Item 240 in the Madisonville Vital Records Department. Solemnized by Isaac H. Henry. Attested by C. R. Cardwell and Harvey Graham (father of bride). Groom age 22; bride age 22. Marriage to occur at Bride's Home. Witnessed by William Bailey and Joseph Cardwell (brother to groom).

3. B640, Book, The Ashby Book, L. F. Reese, 1976, Covers descendants of Henry ASHBY, his will. Also Sinah ASHBY and Reuben BERRY. Connects Joseph ROBERTSON, Sinah BERRY, and Eliz McGARY, pages 741-743, 866-867, Also see B110, page 887.

4. B089, Cemetery Records, from the White School House Cemetery, Volume 3, Hopkins County Cemetery Records in Madisonville, KY, showing members of the Harvey GRAHAM family. C. R. CARDWELL married Emily Clay GRAHAM, who is shown as: E. C., wife of C. B. (R) Cardwell, July 30, 1852-1879. Also shows second son, Thomas K. who lived for 6 months to February 8, 1879. page 120.

5. B123, Marriage Bond, Charles Rice CARDWELL and Fannie BAKER on March 25, 1880. Identifies C. R. Cardwell as principal and C. B. Baker as surety for $100. Groom is 26, Bride is 20. Marriage to occur at the residence of the Bride's mother.

Let me show you how I prepare the software version of a Source. As can be seen below, I start with the sequential number that was assigned to the document, in this case B496. So that document is the 496th of documents related to the Bourlands. This in my software I called *File Number* (see below).

The next is *File Type*. So I select from my taxonomy of Sources the description of the document, in this case a Probate record. Others might be a birth certificate, death certificate, obituary, marriage license, etc. The balance of the information goes on to explain what the document describes, where to find it and so forth.

File Number	B46
File Type	Probate
Book/Periodical	Probate-Saline County, IL, Boxes 17-32
Publisher Name	Saline County Genealogical Society, undated
Comment	Land transaction and Bill for Specific Performance
Comment	for Isaac MASON, which document names wife Lydia and all children, including Martha Mason Bourland

The more Sources you can find for an event such as a birth, the stronger your case for the accuracy of the data. If there are several Sources and they vary for example in date, you need to explain by what reasoning you chose the date presented. It is important to understand that every data field such as birth date requires a Source. The Source is for the field, not the person.

If you fail to follow the above advice, I will promise either you or someone you are working and researching with will ask the by then unanswerable and embarrassing question, "Where did you see/find that?"

There are moments in genealogy where the data does not directly support a conclusion you have drawn. It is appropriate that you share your logic and the conclusion you have drawn in the Notes section of your software.

Chapter Five

WHAT YOUR 2-300 COLLEAGUES MIGHT SEND YOU

Now we return to your Goal to get at least 2-300 researchers or Colleagues to assist in your research. What these Colleagues might send you will vary greatly. Sometimes they will type only a note to the effect that they are trying to prove that Henry X was in and around County Y in about 1825. This may be useful and maybe not; but don't forget, some months later they may have discovered a treasure trove of data on Henry X.

In other cases they may send you a Descendants Report where the children of a couple are lined up under the parents, and so on down the line, usually only with birth and death dates. I find this report barely useful and ask the person if they will send a Register Report with all of their Notes.

A Register Report is the generally accepted and professionally acclaimed method of communicating genealogical data. It was invented some twenty years ago by the New England Historical and Genealogical Society (NEHGS), the oldest such society in the nation. Here is what a Register Report looks like; you will notice it starts with a parent and continues down with each child, generation by generation. The GGG Grandmother is the relationship of that person to me, the owner of the database.

REGISTER REPORT
First Generation

---

1. **Rachel David,** GGG Grandmother. Born abt 1753 in Kent Cty, DE. Rachel died in Fayette Cty, PA, bef 11 May 1801; she was 48.

abt 1782 when Rachel was 29, she first married **James Darling**, GGG Grandfather, son of James Darling & Mary Lnu. Born abt 1754. James died in Duck Creek Hundred, Kent Cty, DE, in 1796; he was 42.

They had the following children:

2	i.	John Darling (1784->1871)
3	ii.	James Darling (~1787->1871)
4	iii.	Eleanor Darling (~1788-)

Second Generation

Family of Rachel David (1) & James Darling

2. **John Darling** (Rachel David1), GGG Uncle. Born in 1784/1785 in Kent Cty, DE. John died aft 9 Mar 1871; he was 87. John was buried in West Liberty, Ohio Cty, WV.

3. **James Darling** (Rachel David1), GGG Uncle. Born abt 1787 in Kent Cty, DE. James died aft 9 Mar 1871; he was 84. James was buried in West Liberty, Ohio Cty, WV.

This Register Report continues down through all generations for which there are data available in a database or for as many generations as you request.

Your Colleague may send you what is called an Ahnentafel Report. Ahnentafel is a German word for "ancestor table." Whereas the Register Report goes down the generations, the Ahnentafel goes up from a person to each of his/her ancestors.

My software allows me to designate a Source and, as you might expect, it is yours truly. So the ensuing ahnentafel is saying John Hackley, Jr. is my 9th Great Grandfather, and his father is my 10th Great Grandfather.

In an Ahnentafel report you should notice that Person #1 will have a father who is twice Person 1's number, and his mother is twice plus 1. So let's say you are looking at a voluminous report at Person #500: his son will be #250 and his father will be #1000. His mother will be #1001.

AHNENTAFEL REPORT
Source

---

1. **John Hackley Jr**, 9G Grandfather. Born abt 1605 in Niton Parish, Isle of Wight, England.
On 10 Oct 1626 when John was 21, he married **Elizabeth Chickle**, 9G Grandmother in England.

They had the following child:
       i.   Richard (~1627-)

Parents

---

2 **John Hackley Sr,** 10G Grandfather. Born abt 1567 in Calbourne Parish, Isle of Wight, England. John died in England in 1640-1661; he was 73.

John married **Annis "Agnes" Granger,** 10G Grandmother.
They had the following children:
      i.   Anne (~1572-)
     ii.   David (~1573-)
    iii.   Joane (~1577-)

3 **Annis "Agnes" Granger**, 10G Grandmother. Born abt 1567 in England. Annis "Agnes" died in England Bet 1578-1668; she was 101.

Grandparents

---

4 **Henry Hackley**, 11G Grandfather. Born abt 1535 in Isle of Wight, England. Henry died in Isle of Wight, England, in 1540-1632.

It is possible you might get other types of reports from your corresponding Colleagues, but generally it will be one of those mentioned above.

If you were lucky, your Colleague might send you a recording or typed version of an interview held between two family members. These can be gold mines of family lore and family history.

ORGANIZING YOUR DATA

We now have some decisions to make.

You should decide on how you file Source material. In my case and with no good reason other than the ability to concentrate on only one family or another, I choose a B Group for my father's name (Bourland) and a W Group for my mother's name

(White). Thus, for every Source item I found I put a sequential number like B001 if it was from my father's line and a W101 if it was my mother's line. So a typical source for me would be:

B678, Marriage License, Isaac MASON and Sally T. RICE on 11 Oct 1806 in Davidson County, TN with a $1,200 bond placed by Isaac Mason and Ebenezer Rice, both of who signed the document. This is a certified copy. Also posted in the Davidson County Marriage Record Book 1, December 13, 1788 to December 29, 1837, page number 5.

B678 is the 678th document in my father's line; it is a Marriage license as described for Isaac Mason and Sally Rice. Plan ahead, use 4 digit numbers, B0001.

You may be tempted to file all your marriage licenses or probate records together. Don't. Think what a time you would have searching through 100 licenses to find the one you want. And how would you file them, by alphabet of bride? of groom? Pastor? Do you see the problem?

Next you must decide on what and how you maintain your records. In my case I said I will give it a number (B0002) if I have a copy in my work-papers, that is, in my legal folders with a sequentially numbered label.

If I do not have the actual document, but consider the fact important, I would merely mention it in the Notes of my database. So, if someone tells me something, and there is a chance it is true or it is rather interesting, I would have a Note in my database that says, "Bob Smith of Fort Smith, AK and BSmith@aol.com related by telephone (so no hardcopy) that Henry was once arrested for drunkenness."

So if it has a number, there is a physical manifestation in my workpapers with a number such as B1003. You of course will set your own rules.

Lastly, we must decide what to do with pictures. These might be modern day digital pictures, or might be a photograph of a scanned picture from a newspaper article. A good decision is to use the number the computer assigns to every person in your database (sometimes called an ID Number or Person Number or some such). That way whenever you call that person into a report you can show his ID number, and his photo can be found in an electronic Picture Folder where all electronic pictures are kept, named as:

#2188 John Bobbitt
#2306 William Cardwell, on horse

Sometimes we are not certain of the identity of the subjects of a critical photograph. Maureen Taylor at www.photodetective.com is experienced at analyzing photographs and determining the period from clothing, store and street signs, the photographer's name and so forth and may be able to help, for a fee.

Now to lighten up a bit, before reviewing:

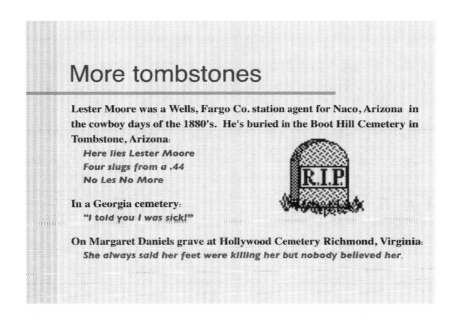

To again insure we continue on the right path, let us review the **Work Plan** steps that have been identified since Chapter 2:

- Learn about and use http://wc.rootsweb.ancestry.com

- Begin to collect, document in a spreadsheet or other listing and work with 2-300 Colleagues, particularly those you identify from their postings on the Internet

- Go to www.rootsweb.com and search your Surnames; sign up for each Surname List and review Archives; go to each County and State of interest and collect more Colleagues

- Go to and enroll in each County web site of interest

- Google search your surname(s)

- Document your Sources, remembering Elizabeth Mills' *Evidence! Citation and Analysis for the Family Historian*

- Insure you know how to use Sources in your software

- Insure knowledge of Register Report

- Insure knowledge of Ahnentafel Report

- Organize your data for easy retrieval, label and file

- Number important pictures with Person Number from software

We will now continue with the next steps in the Work Plan. The next such review will be found in Chapter 9.

Chapter Six

VISIT SITES – CITIES, COUNTIES, LIBRARIES, HISTORICAL & GENEALOGY SOCIETIES

The Internet contains an ever increasing amount of genealogical data. If you live in a large city the local library can also contain a great deal of useful information. But it is eventually critical that you visit the town where you grew up and more importantly the towns where your parents and grandparents were raised. Sometimes the County is more important than the town as a source of data. So you must visit the town, the county, and the libraries of each.

Many towns have in addition a **Genealogical Society** and/or an **Historical Society** and they are clearly worth a visit. In each you should ask if there is a **Mugbook**, so called because there are usually pictures and write-ups on many persons and families. In the 1980s there were several companies that traveled to many cities and requested the natives to submit genealogical information. The company then published a book, which in the case related to my search was entitled *The Heritage of Hopkins County, Kentucky 1807-1987*. It was published by Turner Publishing. Their current web site is located at **www.turnerpublishing.com**. You should search this site to see if there are books for your areas of interest. In addition, **www.Newberry. org** and **www.Higginsonbooks.com** also have certain Mugbooks.

When you visit these cities or counties, you should attempt to locate possible relatives (cousins) using the telephone book or lists maintained by researchers in the various Societies. You may as I did meet many new cousins and find a Colleague. While in the city/county, pick up a telephone book for your own use as you will find yourself calling back cousins (?) who were not available while you were there. This will save you time finding their telephone number.

But, be sure you plan ahead. Several times I have gone to a Society to learn they were only open on certain days or hours. Sometimes the Librarian was unaware there even was a Genealogy group. Therefore, you should Google the town, call the library and societies before going and then map out a strategy to maximize your time and effort.

A description of my second visit to the birthplace of my father, Hopkins County, KY, may be instructive. I had failed to "plan ahead" on my first visit! I went first to the library, asked for and located the Genealogy Society room. It was locked and I was not a member. I asked who the president or active member was and called him. He authorized my entrance and later took my membership in the Society. While there I:

- Reviewed probably 250 family histories for those surnames in which I was or became interested;

- Reviewed a Register of members and the surnames in which they were interested. Called each of them with my surnames, and those not at home I called later on back in St. Louis where I lived using a telephone book I had appropriated;

- Reviewed various books, a Mugbook (see above) and pamphlets;

- Determined which newspapers existed in the past and where copies could be located;

- Located and visited the Historical Society. Looked at their library and other materials. Introduced myself to the curators and recorded their names and phone number;

- Looked in every room, in every bookcase, in every cabinet and located a true serendipity: the former president had cut every personal item from all three newspapers for the period from 1890s to 1980s, pasted them to 8½ X 11 pages and put them alphabetically in 3-ring binders. Wow, did I get many, many items of local color for the Notes in my database. The curators were unaware of the existence of these 10 binders;

I trust you are noticing the aggressive nature of my search; calling someone to be let into the Genealogy room; opening every door and cabinet to find the binders. By aggressive I do not mean intrusive or offensive, but knowing what I wanted and setting out to find it. Continuing ....

- Picked up a telephone book to take back home;

- Went to the town cemeteries, talked with the front desks for information and took pictures of known markers; wrote down family members buried nearby whose names I did not know for later research;

- Met with several new cousins which had been identified and copied their books, notes and so forth by going to a local print shop;

- Went to the town schools to seek Yearbooks and grades and reports on my immediate family;

- Identified for the next day a review of past issues of their Newsletter, one seen partially below;

- Identified for the next day a review of past issues of their Newsletter, one seen partially below;

YESTERDAY'S TUCKAWAYS

© HOPKINS CO. GENEALOGICAL SOCIETY, INC. • PO BOX 51 • MADISONVILLE, KY 42431
VOLUME 40 NO. 2   SUMMER 2008

Note from the President

After holding office in Hopkins County Genealogical Society for several years, I am resigning as President in August of this year to return to college. I want to thank the members for their support, help, and encouragement. The Society is to be commended for the projects they have completed during this time and for continuing to offer such a large and useful collection of reference material for genealogical researchers.

Vice-President Jane Ann Jackson will be Acting President from August 1, 2008 until the election of officers for 2009. She brings business experience and leadership abilities to the office of President as well as a sincere interest in the Society. Please give her the same support and cooperation I have always enjoyed as President.

Sincerely, Betty Cox.

New Books for Sale

Hopkins County Genealogical Society has

Reid-Walters Funeral Home Records

This book of Reid-Walters burials is available for $20.00 plus $3.00 shipping.

If both books are purchased together, shipping will be only $4.00.

Hopkins County College Students in 1949

Thanks to Tom Clinton, Editor of The Messenger, for permission to print these vintage articles. This abstracted information is from an article in The Messenger; Sept. 28, 1949, about students leaving for college.

Bowling Green Business University

Edwin & Jesse McGary, (Junior class); sons of Jesse McGary.

In This Issue

Then I wrote a Trip Report, one such partially seen below, so that I could remember what I did and did not finish, those I met and other unfinished or completed efforts.

Trip Report

C. R. Bourland, Jr.   Madisonville, KY   1/16/1996 to 1/18/96

The following is a report on a trip taken by C. R. Bourland to visit Madisonville, KY; this the second such trip.

Called D.P. Duncan, cousin, friend and President of the Genealogy Society to confirm the room in the Library would be open; he said yes. I arrived to find it closed due to Martin Luther King's birthday. Next time call ahead.

Visited the Vital Records department in the Courthouse and obtained some marriage records. While style of record keeping changed in about 1868 (from "I married them" to "this is who they are and their parents and in their home I married them"), this may be the best record keeping Duncan and certainly I have ever seen for bureaucrats. Got Pidcock and Fannie Cardwell and other records.

Went to Grapevine Cemetery but it was closed. Again, call ahead. Went to the Odd Fellows Cemetery and toured around by car, there being less interest than in Grapevine. Later I learned the Baker's are all here. Then across the street to Duncans and picked up two books on Bobbitts for reproduction. Went to Happy's across the street from the Library where I copied both books.

Went down N. Seminary to find 255 and 435, the latter now the Kentucky Health Center for long-term care. Talked with Mr. Blecher the chief Administrator, who does not know much of the history. So the family lived until about 1940 at 435 and then went to 255, probably at Pop's death. Talked with Mr. and Mrs. Muller who bought the house at auction in 1976. They remember Eliz and Pidcock and that there were pins all over the house.

Registered at the Day's End Motel, an ok and inexpensive place. Had dinner at Beauregard's next door to the Library. Etc, etc.

The Mugbook was out of print and I did not have time to copy it. Much later I identified a cousin in San Francisco who volunteered to send/lend it to me so that

I might copy it.

And this is a good time to emphasize that the genealogical community is one that shares graciously and quickly. This is one reason why I wrote the book on some 100 families called *Miscellaneous Hopkins County Families*, to pay back the many courtesies I received over the years as part of this "community" generosity. There may be other libraries in your area, including state or private universities, which should be visited.

As an aside, which may serve to motivate you, my wife and I took these "field trips" for a few years and they remain some of our most rewarding travel memories. We have been lucky to be able to travel to many exotic, foreign destinations but what we learned and savored during the genealogy-related trips has been very special. Front porch conversations over iced tea with distant cousins, slice-of-Americana lunches at courthouse square diners, microfilm research at imposing, all-marble federal buildings in Washington, D.C., poring over shelves of three-ring binders painstakingly assembled by hand in the dining room of a small farm house in the Midwest, a long table groaning with many lovingly prepared family recipes presented with pride at an annual family reunion ... too many eye-opening, touching and fun memories to list here. Above all, the many different but unfailingly kind and welcoming total strangers who opened their doors and stories wide for us without any hesitation!

Some particular excellent libraries that may not be in your area but should be visited in person or visited via the Internet include:

Allen County Public Library-Fort Wayne, Indiana:

The renowned Allen County Public Library has grown since 1895 to a main library in downtown Fort Wayne, IN.

The Library's Genealogical Center contains more than 350,000 printed volumes and 513,000 items of microfilm and microfiche. Their collection includes over 50,000 volumes of compiled genealogies on American and European families. It is a cooperating partner with the Family History Library in Salt Lake City.
In addition, they are active in initiatives to make significant public domain portions of its collection available on-line, including contributions to **www.Footnote.com**

and other digitized family history efforts.

The Library in concert with Brigham Young University and the Mormon Church (see later) is in the process of making several thousands of genealogy books available on line in a searchable database.

Their web address is: **www.acpl.lib.in.us.** They have a searchable surname system at: **www.genealogycenter.info.** Their address is: Allen County Public Library, Fort Wayne IN 46802, Phone (260) 421-1200.

Brigham Young University, Harold B. Lee Library:

This library in concert with the Mormon Church and the Allen County (IN) Public Library is in the process of making several thousands of genealogy books available on-line in a searchable database.

Their Harold B. Lee Library should be extensively searched for valuable information. In addition, their Family History Archive and other locations at the below web address are important sites to visit. The web address is **www.lib.byu.edu.**

Related useful sites are **www.Immigrants.byu.edu**, which is tracking people and vessels with immigrants into America, and **www.Scripts.byu.edu** which is establishing a site to translate Old German, Dutch, French, Italian, Portuguese and Spanish documents.

Jesus Christ of the Latter Day Saints (Mormons in Salt Lake City):

The Latter Day Saints have resource centers in 4,500 family history centers in 70 countries, including the large Family History Center in Salt Lake City.

Their web site is increasingly important, especially as they computerize thousands of family histories and related items. Patrons may access their web site through **www.FamilySearch.org.**

They offer a free software system for genealogy called the Personal Ancestral File (PAF). They also have the International Genealogical Index (IGI) that can assist in locating immigrant ancestors from foreign countries, especially Europe.

The Church in concert with Brigham Young University and the Allen County (IN) Public Library is in the process of making several thousands of genealogy books available on line in a searchable database.

Ladson Genealogical Library in Vidalia, Georgia:

The Ladson Genealogical Library collection comprises more than 30,000 books and pamphlets as well as manuscripts and microfilm, covering state and county histories, marriage and death records, Census and church records, Confederate rosters, individual biographies, family histories, genealogical periodicals and materials on heraldry. The library is a branch of the Vidalia-Toombs County Library, part of the Ohoopee Regional Library System. Its web address is: **www.ohoopeelibrary.org/ladson.htm**. Their address is: Vidalia, Georgia 30474 Phone: (912) 537-8186

New England Historic Genealogical Society (NEHGS):

If you have any connection whatsoever to the New England states they will be well advised to join for $75 annually (currently) as their data is priceless. Their Great Migration Study for an additional $20 annually is well on its way to an intensive study of all immigrants to America between 1620 to 1643 into New England states. They have published the New England Historical and Genealogical Register (NEHGR) since 1847 in quarterly issues with articles tracking a family or issue of interest. Their database includes more than 110,000,000 names in 2,200

New England Historic & Genealogical Society (NEHGS)

- Register - NEHGR - 1847- 2001-Today
- 110,000,000 names
- 2,200 databases
- 200,000 books
- Classes
- Trips - Salt Lake City Mormons
- Great Migration Study Project
  - Robert Charles Anderson
  - 1620 - 1643

databases. They conduct numerous classes and manage trips to Salt Lake City, to Europe and numerous other historic places as well. Their web address is **www. newenglandancestors.org.**

Lastly, in many cities there are Genealogical and Historical Associations or Societies that meet monthly or to their own schedule and there one can find many who can assist with the local and state repositories.

Let us review, in the slide and below:

Let's review

- Record & maintain Sources
- Visit City/County/State
  - Mugbook
    - TurnerPublishing.com
    - Newberry.org
    - Higginsonbooks.com
  - Telephone book
- Join Ancestry.com and NEHGS
- Genealogical Libraries
- Signup for rootsweb.com
  - Surnames, State, County

We have discussed Sources; the necessity to physically visit the cities of you, your parents and others where much can be found; Mugbooks; and a variety of important genealogical libraries beyond your home city.

In addition, here is a reminder to join Ancestry.com and NEHGS.

Here also is a strong reminder to sign up at **www.rootsweb.com** where you can collect valuable information and many Colleagues.

Chapter Seven

USE YOUR SOFTWARE and PREPARE FOR FINAL PRODUCT

I find that many people are somewhat reluctant to get into a piece of software such as one for genealogy. They sometimes come with a rather thick manual, and thus are imposing. Other people jump right in.

For those who are not jumpers, here are my thoughts. First, if at any time you are unsure where to find something or are lost on what to do next, call the vendor's Help Line. I have yet to hear of a vendor of this kind of software who is unconcerned and all are anxious to earn reference sales from your friends. **So call the vendor if you are having trouble.**

Next, almost all software starts with a screen for a husband and wife, usually displaying both sets of parents and children. Surely you know the birth dates and places of you and your spouse, as well as your children. It may take a few minutes to find it but you can easily locate the birth/death dates of your parents and grandparents. (If you are lucky enough that they are still living, they can tell you of those dates and places for their parents, your grandparents). So already you have a database of perhaps 10-20 people.

Don't worry about your siblings, your Uncles, Aunts and First Cousins - just get started by entering the data for the first 10-20 or so.

Now you probably have your own birth certificate, used to vote or obtain a passport. This can be your first Source document. Place your sequentially numbered label on it, and put it in a legal folder. Enter it next into your software and you now know where and how to enter those all-important Source documents. Here is one, not very informative but actual:

B1092, Birth Certificate, for Tyler Ryan, May 1, 2008, State File Number: 109-2008-068374.

Here's another, more informative, and actual:

B723, Birth Certificate, Valerie Sue Smith on February 25, 1935 at the Quintard Hospital, San Diego, California. Parents: Brick Smith, age 34, and Helen Lucile Jones, age 22. Birth occurred at 6:27 a.m. with Dr. D. H. Warner attending.

If you have a handy picture of yourself, obtain the digital version or scan it into your computer. Assuming you put yourself into the software first and thus have been assigned the number "1," open a Folder named Family Pictures and put your photograph in labeled "#0001 Your Name."

Next, find the area in the software where reports are located and see if you have one called Register Report. It might be called Descendants Report or similar. Now go to the top, that is the oldest person in one of your families and run the report starting with him/her. It should look like the report on page 29.

If all is running smoothly, go back and add such data as your software describes (some software allows you to self describe these data) under special headings such as Occupation, Religion, Cause of Death and Education.

Lastly in this sequence, get from your files or create a small resumé in Word or whatever word-processor you use. When you have perhaps a half page worth, copy and paste it into the Notes section of your genealogy software. This gives you practice in obtaining data from relatives, the Internet, books or the like and bringing them into the "book" you are writing. Put all such data in chronological order, in well written paragraph form, ready for your book.

By the way, the Register Report you did earlier, with the addition of the biography you put together can be called a "small book," do you not agree?

Now go back to your Person screens and start not with the oldest person but the youngest, which may be you or may be a child. Find a report entitled "Ahnentafel" and run that report. What you will get is a report similar to that on page 30 that will provide all ancestors in the database for the selected person (you or the child).

The intention here is not to cover all aspects of your genealogy software – that is best left to its vendor. But if you follow the above steps, you will be well on your way to competency and in addition you will be quickly over your fear of the unknown.

Let me emphasize, if you are having trouble, **CALL THE HELP DESK OF THE VENDOR.** But start as soon as possible on learning about and entering some data into the software so that you are comfortable in so doing.

Once again we return to the Work Plan, and see that we have been through the following steps or tasks.

Work Plan, continued

- Work "known" to "unknown"   √
- Use a wide focus   √
- Document your sources   √
- Organize your data   √
- Visit sites   √
  - Cities, Counties
  - Libraries, Historical and Genealogical Societies

What To Do With Surnames That Are "Maybes"

In the course of your research you will find data on a surname about which you remain uncertain if it is your family. You will also come across data that looks interesting for a host of reasons, but you know better than to add such to your database as it is but a guess. So you take notes and place them in a manila folder appropriately labeled. There is an established method of recording that data, aside from a note written to yourself.

The method looks like this:

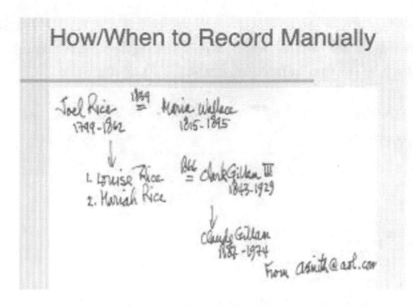

How/When to Record Manually

As you see, you place husband and wife together as shown and include under them their dates. The = sign represents a marriage and the date above the = sign is the date of the marriage. The downward arrow suggests a child, Louisa, and the second child is named Mariah but in this case we have found data only on Louisa, or we are only interested in Louisa. She was married in turn to Clark Gillham, III.

Lastly, one would place the Source on the document, seen bottom right in the example.

FINAL PRODUCT

It is time to discuss important aspects of your final product.

Presumably at this point you have become experienced with Register Reports and Ahnentafels. You are reasonably competent in Word. You have learned perhaps that your genealogical software provides your reports with an extension of ".rtf." You know this stands for Rich Text Format but you also know you should open the ".rtf "and (re)Save As ".doc." This of course is a normal Word document that can be easily manipulated.

If you are not interested in leaving something for posterity, just keep researching. But, if you have accepted my challenge of writing a book and as Zola said '*that is a full life*', let's think ahead to what we wish to do and how.

You may or may not have put your autobiography in the Notes section of the software. I wrote my autobiography only for my direct descendants and not for the broad family for whom I wrote the books on page 4. For the same reason I also did not put my father's autobiography in the Notes section. Had I been successful in getting my mother to write her autobiography, it too would not have gone to the Notes. I wrote instead a rather brief biography for me and my parents for the Notes.

I placed the more elaborate and hence more personal autobiographies in a separate book I called Bourland Personal, along with other writings in which cousins would not be interested, such as Vacation Diaries, Extensive Interviews, Reflections on my Sons and so forth. See page 5.

You will have your own ambitions and thoughts here, which most likely will differ from mine, and you should begin to think about them.

These are the some of the decisions to be made, Register?, Ahnentafel?, and so forth.

If you decide on a Register Report format, it may look like the following.

GUY-TAINTOR CHAPTER
First Generation

---

1. Nicholas Guy Sr, 10G Grandfather. Buried on 9 Jan 1633.

Nicholas Guy sailed from Southampton for New England 24 April 1638 on the *Confidence* of London

On 11 May 1578 Nicholas married Margaret Seward, 10G Grandmother.

They had the following children:
2   i.   Nicholas (~1586-1649)
*   ii.   Margaret, 10G Aunt. Margaret was baptized on 15 Nov 1594.*

Family of Nicholas Guy Sr (1) & Margaret Seward

2. Deacon Nicholas Guy Jr (Nicholas1), 9G Grandfather. Born abt 1586 in Upton Gray, Hants, England. Nicholas was baptized in Upton Gray, Hants, England, on 10 Jan 1586. Nicholas died on 1 Jul 1649 in Watertown, Middlesex Cty, MA. Occupation: Carpenter.

Nicholas, Jane Guy and daughter Mary (Joseph Tainter's future wife) were once members of the Upton-Gray Church, Hampshire, England, near Basingstoke. Jane was Nicholas' second wife and stepmother to Mary. Joseph Tainter, as an employee of Nicholas, may also have attended that church before they departed from Southampton, Hampshire, England for the Massachusetts Colony on 24 April 1638 on the ship Confidence of London (Verified by passenger manifest maintained at the PRO at Kew, a suburb of London.)

The following is a local Edinburgh, Scotland encyclopedia (quaint to Americans) account concerning Upton-Gray: Upton-Gray, a parish, in the union of Basingstoke, hundred of Bermondspit, Basingstoke and N. divisions of the county of Southampton, 4 miles (W.S.W.) from Odiham; containing, with the tything of Hoddington, 504 inhabitants. The living is a perpetual curacy, in the gift of Queen's College, Oxford: the impropriate tithes have been commuted for £490, and there are 49 acres of impropriate glebe.

You would see (if this book were in color) that I decided to take the standard Register Report output from my genealogy software which comes out in Word and doctor it up a bit. I made all the Males appear in Blue color and the Females in Red (colors not shown here). Also, I extracted some of the major highlights and placed them into a box in red. This was done, of course, to bring attention to the fact but also to break up the writing with the closest thing to a picture possible. As they say, a picture is worth 1000 words. If a picture were available, it would be inserted into the Word document. In some cases a graphics cartoon might be useful and many of these can be found on the Internet and in word processor software.

If on the other hand you would choose to prepare an Ahnentafel for your book, it would look like the illustration on page 30. An Ahnentafel can be somewhat

Decide on Recording Formats

- Facts or Paragraphs
- In date sequence or as found
- Paragraphs indented or not
- Abbreviations - Co, IL, 5 Jun 1978
- Determine county or not
- Punctuation or not, as in name - Mary A Smith
- Name in caps
- Middle name in full or initial
- Unrelated history or not

confusing and thus, except in the rare case, is not as useful and readable as a Register Report. It does, however, expose all ancestors you have for a person. This type of report allows a reader, for example, to see all of the 6th great grandparents at once, or at least in the same section of the book.

And it is possible you have researched one special person and you wish to write about his or her life. You may wish to write a novel and create possible events in the life of a person or a family. Regardless, you will have met the Objective – a book.

Since you have given thought to what your final output will be, there are some decisions you should make up front based on that decision. And by the way, that decision is not irrevocable, as I found out.

Some people just state a fact in their Notes. Example: Joseph born 1.6.1845. Since I wanted to write a book, an example in my case might be: *Their first son Joseph was born on January 6, 1845. They were happy parents and looked forward to a second child, Helen, to be born shortly thereafter.*

Do you put facts into the Notes as you find them, or do you bother to put them into date sequence? I chose sequenced by date. Do you indent paragraphs or not? I did not because one often decides to change the first line of a paragraph.

Do you abbreviate or not? I abbreviated states as KY, and I did the same for County, but used "Cty" to avoid confusion. In fact, you should decide if you will bother to look up the county since most often it is not provided with a place, though easily found through Google.

Do you use punctuation in a name? I use no punctuation, thus Mary A Smith. In this same regard, many people use upper case for last name because it makes the surname stand out in a reading. I find it distracting and so use initial cap only, as John A Smith, not John A SMITH. Either way is fine.

Do you use middle name in full or with initial? I recommend full middle name if available since most often it ties to a parent or grandparent surname.

Lastly, I recommend you add interesting historical facts or observations as they are appropriate and as you find them. For example, here are three I chose to place in an appropriate Note:

"It was a propitious year as seen in this record from the Hustler: By means of the wonderful long distance telephone, people in Madisonville can now talk with people at Hopkinsville, Nashville, Henderson, Evansville and intermediate points, and the conversation can be as distinctly understood as if the persons conversing were within a few feet of one another. The route will be extended to Louisville in the spring. [4 Jan 1895 Hustler] My father's birth year was thusly celebrated."

"The given name Leonidas may well come from the family's reading of the classics, wherein Leonidas of Rhodes was an Olympian runner who won all three races for four consecutive Olympics starting in 164 B.C."

"In those days the railroad tracks above the Ohio River were 4'9" while those below were 5' wide. Through cars were hoisted to have their wheels changed at Henderson."

I also used as a Note descriptions of the Mexican conflict prior to WW1 (The Mexican Punitive Expedition of 1916-1917) and the War of 1812 because few are conversant with them and certainly not my grandchildren. Both events had participants to whom I am related.

Another break:

More tombstones

On a grave from the 1880's in Nantucket, Massachusetts:
Under the sod and under the trees
Lies the body of Jonathan Pease.
He is not here, there's only the pod:
Pease shelled out and went to God.

In a Thurmont, Maryland cemetery:
Here lies an Atheist
All dressed up
And no place to go.

In another Maryland cemetery:
Here lies Baby Jane
Now she never hollers
She blessed our home for thirty days
And cost us forty dollars

Mistakes I Made

Now is as good a time as ever to discuss **mistakes** I made in my own genealogical efforts. We all make them and you will as well, but none is catastrophic. The discussion to follow will suggest that you need to think about actions you take and their future ramifications.

When I started with my effort, there was a barely functioning Internet, use of the telephone was fairly expensive, no software included a report writer (Register Report) and, finally, genealogy software was pretty basic. Your most important tool, Google, did not exist.

I thought paragraphs would add many pages and thus a book with paragraphs would be more costly than one without. So I ended each prospective paragraph with an exclamation point (!). Then I used my word processor to find each "!" and substitute 15 spaces. The reader would then know by the spaces where a paragraph ended and a new one began. After my first book, I decided this decision was a bad one, and I stopped. I am still removing those pesky "!" marks in some of my older data.

My first software had limited field sizes. A field is "Date", another field is "Birth Place." So I was required to abbreviate some data, such as GrapevineCem,HopkinsCo,KY (sic) instead of Grapevine Cemetery, Hopkins County, KY. To this date I continue to fix these fields using my much improved software.

I found a husband and wife in my research where one was a Bourland and one was a White. Later it was determined I was only related to the Bourland. There are many White families. But I was so excited I took a GEDCOM from them and added it directly and electronically into my database. A GEDCOM will be discussed later but it permits direct entry of another's database into yours. As you would guess, I have in my data about 1,000 names in which I have no interest. But the problem is even greater. I thought their data had an exotic style that did not resemble mine at all. I would say 99.6% of all of my data carries my style on the 56,000 people (except for the oddball 1,000 from a GEDCOM).

When it comes to pictures, I started just naming them. So there are J.M. Smith, Joe Smith, J. Martin Smith pictures and all of the same person. Then I figured out that if I used the Person ID given each person by the genealogy software, I could avoid that problem. So I switched. See page 33 for an example.

Lastly, I messed up by not using a good Sourcing system. My first software system did not have a sourcing system. So I merely buried in the Notes something like "see B0804." Later on, when my software had a proper Sourcing system, I thought it was too complicated and did not use it for several years. Finally a new Colleague convinced me of my error and I switched. Today my truly researched data has a Source for all data, or the notation of its speculation or surmise. Readers can assess the value of my data within the Register Report which includes Endnotes of the Sources for that data.

Sourcing is the imprimatur of an experienced and knowledgeable genealogist. Please, do it correctly; it is worth the effort and lets you know, and others know (which is more important) the value of your work. **Data without the proof of a Source is close to useless.**

Chapter Eight

WHAT TO LOOK AT

We must next explore those data that are key elements to building an accurate knowledge of our ancestors. There are many areas which will bear fruit, but not every time nor for everyone you research. But these areas should be explored not only for basic data but serendipities as well.

Census Records

The first Census was taken in 1790. Before that time and in certain locations one can locate poll tax records or other quasi-governmental records and construct a rudimentary Census. But 1790 was the first official U.S. Census.

What To Look At

- Items of use include:
  - Census records
  - Birth, death records
  - Marriage certificates
  - Wills, Probate records
  - Deeds
  - Cemetery records
  - Obituaries
  - Court records
  - Military and church records, and city directories

The 1890 Census was essentially lost by fire, although again a few locations built a nearly correct Census from tax and other records.

The Census records are available by surname and location on **www.Ancestry.com** as well as **www.HeritageQuest.com**. Many libraries have access to both services, often free to you. Because much of the Census was recorded by semi-educated individuals, the spelling is often phonetic or just plain wrong. If the record is barely readable on one system, you should try the other as it may be more legible.

Generally, when searching Ancestry.com, let's say, if the person or family you seek is not found, you should adjust or shorten the search. What that means is search without one of your criteria such as first name, county, birthplace, year of birth and so forth. Or, if there are many responses, start with just one criteria and then add more to reduce the list.

Census records

- 1790 - the first
- 1800, 1810, 1820,1830,1840 - Sex and age
- 1850,1860,1870,1880 - Occ, r/e, birth place
- 1890 - Mostly lost
- 1900
- 1910
- 1920
- 1930 - home, race, education, occupation, vet

Soundex Codes

Carry a blank copy with you at all times

Some Census recordings (and other genealogy records as well) permit a search by Soundex Number (sometimes called a 'fuzzy search') when the name is complicated. This number is a mathematical representation of the phonetic name. For example, Bourland in Soundex is B645. Cardwell is C634. Do not worry about the formula, those places which permit such a search will provide the result of the formula for you.

As time progressed, the data collected by the Census takers increased. The first 1790 Census gave only the family name and a count by age of the females and males. The 1930 Census goes so far as to indicate whether a radio existed in the home. By law, the Census data must be 70 years old to be available to the public. Thus as of this writing, 1930 is the latest.

As the slide suggests, starting in 1850 one finds occupation, value of real estate and value of other assets. If you are interested in determining the modern day value of those figures, go to *measuringworth.com.*

It is highly recommended that early in your research you obtain a blank copy of each Census form so that you can tell what each value represents from what is at times a most difficult to read computer record.

The Census records represent a Primary Source record of a family at one point in time and will prove extremely useful. Some researchers choose to include the Census record itself into a Note or a folder associated with a Note. Here is what I do with direct family lines, but not most collateral lines: I type as seen below into the Note because I do not wish the reader to have to determine what the microfilm or computer says when I have a better understanding of the data from my research than they ever will:

The 1850 Census shows District 1, #787: David S. Cardwell, 30; Mary A., 25; Henry Ann Kelly (f), 6; Davidella Kelly (f) 3; and Joseph L. Cardwell 11/12. See B046.

The 1860 Census shows David S. Cardwell, age 40, farmer from Kentucky, $1000/0 with the following in the household: Mary, 34, KY; Joseph L.,10, KY; James, 8, KY; Charles E. (sic), 6, KY; Lawrence, 4, KY; John D, 2, KY; David E. Kelly, 14, female; Bennet Brasswell (?), male 24, day laborer; Elizabeth Robertson, 80, $500, $300 KY. See B047.

The 1870 Census shows D. S. Cardwell, age 50 (1820), farmer, p.e. $1,000, KY. with the following household: Mary A., 45, KY; Joseph L, 20, Laborer, KY; James A., 18, Laborer, KY; Charles R., 16, KY; Lawrence, 14, KY; David F., 9; Laura, 7; William H, 5; plus a Rosa Hamby, age 38, Black, domestic servant, born in KY and with a young son named William. See B048.

And sometimes I type in the Notes in the fashion below, but notice that above and below in all cases there is a Source number indicating where the actual copy is in my files. In all cases I have added the probable names:

1820 Census for Waconteby, White County, Illinois   See B711
Males
00-09   2   *William, Cyrus*
10-15   1   *Thomas*
26-44   1   *Isaac is 38 yrs*

Females
00-09   4   *Martha, Sarah, Narcissa, Harriett*
26-44   1   *Sarah "Sally" Rice Mason is 32 yrs*

1830 Census for Equality, Gallatin County, Illinois   See B715
Males
00-04   1   *Cyrus*
05-09   1   *??*
10-14   1   *William*
20-29   2   *Thomas, Unknown*

40-49   1   Isaac is 48 yrs

Females
10-14   4   Harriett
40-49   1   Sarah "Sally" T. Rice Mason is 42 yrs

We talked earlier about using a wide focus. That is, capturing such people as godparents, inventory takers, neighbors and so forth. Following is one example in my Notes from one Census record:

In this 1850 Census there are several related families living contiguously:

Household #50 has Jonathan B. Moore, son of Allen Floyd Moore who married Sally T. Rice's half-sister, Martha Rice. Harriett Bays is in this home;

Household #51 is Benjamin Magnes Carnahan son of James Carnahan/Mary Slaton where Mary married (2) David Bays, Jr. (after (1) Sarah Louise Mason, daughter of Isaac Mason, died) and in addition Benjamin's sister Elizabeth married Ebenezer Franklin Bourland and further Benjamin's sister Phoebe married Rev Ebenezer R. Moore whose mother was Martha Rice Moore and Ebenezer administered Isaac Mason's probate and further Benjamin's sister Lucinda married Jonathan B. Moore, son of Martha Rice Moore;

Household #52 is Isaac Mason, Jr.;

Household #53 is William M. Mason, son of Isaac. Harriett Bourland and Frederick, Thomas and Columbus Maltby are in this home;

Household #54 is John Jackson Slaton, brother to Mary who married (2) David Bays, and he himself is married to Hannah Roark, daughter of Michael Roark and further his sister Rachel Slaton married William G. Bourland;

Household #55 is Thomas Delaney Carnahan, son of James Carnahan/Mary Slaton, the latter who married (2) David Bays;

Household #56 is Michael Roark, father to Hannah before, and whose son William married Muhulda Bourland and whose daughter Nancy married Israel D. Sisk. Isaac D. Maltby is in this home.

Imagine this serendipitous finding - seven homes with relatives living contiguously.

Birth Records

Birth records vary widely by city, county and state. Some have considerable data such as occupation of the parents, time of birth, certain medical procedures performed such as silver nitrate for the eyes and the like. Other places may provide only the very basic information.

The book *Handybook for Genealogists*, which by now should be in your personal library, lists who such as County Clerk or Health Department or other has what records, their telephone number, their address, and so forth for every county in the nation, if available.

Do not be surprised at what you find; for example, Kentucky did not require birth records until 1911. Counties and States will vary all over the lot. In many cases you will have to arrive at a birth or death date from Census records. You may need to compare successive Census records as the date of the Census may vary from one to the other and the age of a person may vary slightly. In these case it is normal to write "born about such and such date", or you will often see "abt 1824."

Death Records

Once again the *Handybook for Genealogists* provides the who, where and address with telephone number for death records. These records will vary in terms of the amount of information provided and are valuable providers of useful data such as cause of death and occupation, etc. Often a probate record or legal record is the only source of a death date, or estimation of that date.

Marriage Records

With marriage records you will find a great variety of styles. Some places have well-kept Registers with dates, bride and groom names as well as officiating person, preacher, Justice of the Peace or other. Some places have turned that data into an electronic record which can be searched; but remember, that would be a Secondary

Source and not a Primary as the actual document would be.

In some places back in time you will find scraps of paper, as shown. In yet another case you may find a list of marriages in a year, also shown.

In the "scrap of paper" example, I printed a translation under the copy of the document to save the reader the effort. Next is a year-long list of marriages a particular Reverend performed.

Wills, Probate Records and Court Cases

Wills are a most valuable source of information to help you determine family structure, wealth, friends and neighbors, who may sooner or later become relatives.

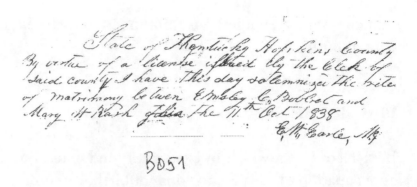

B051

STATE OF KENTUCKY HOPKINS COUNTY

BY VIRTUE OF A LICENSE ISSUED BY THE CLERK OF SAID COUNTY I HAVE THIS DAY SOLEMNIZED THE RITES OF MATRIMONY BETWEEN EMSLEY C. BOBBIT AND MARY AN RASH THIS THE 11th OCT 1838

E. M. EARLE

Structure comes from the naming of a wife, a list of children (although not necessarily all as some may have left the area or have received an inheritance earlier), the married name of daughters and the first name of daughters-in-law and, from the witness list, possible friends and maybe a future or present son-in-law.

When a will is probated, the estate is normally inventoried and again one can find friends and relatives listed. The inventory can help one write reasonable speculations on the occupation, lifestyle and much more. Here is an excerpt from one such analysis:

.... *First of all, I organized all of the items listed in the inventory into five categories and tabulated the listed value for each category with the following results:*
 1) Livestock = 23% of total
   (49 animals which included horses, cows, pigs, sheep and geese)
 2) Crops/Products = 4%
   (rye, corn, flax and wool)
 3) Slaves = 58%
   (two slaves)
 4) Household Items = 9%
   (furniture, kitchen utensils)
 5) Farm Equipment = 6%
   (tools and other stuff)

By far, the most valuable items of personal property were the slaves. Individually they were more valuable than any other item, and combined, they formed over half of the total value of the physical property items. The next most valuable category was the livestock, which was worth almost one fourth of the entire moveable property value, belying their survival value for a pioneer life style. And he did have a lot of animals! 5 geese, 2 horses, 6 sheep, 22 pigs and 14 cows 49 in all if my math is right.

There is more in this analysis, but this will give you the flavor of it.

I will include one more record, in this case a "Bill for Specific Performance" to dramatize that useful information can be found in many places. This is an illustration of a Court Case.

Hezikiah Hargrave vs Lydia Gossit etal; box C-14
File June 1857   Bill for Specific Performance. ...
Your, Orator, Hezekiah Hargrave, would represent on the 9th day of Feb., he purchased from Isaac Mason the following described tracts of land situated in the Saline County, to wit: The SW 1/4 SW 1/4 SEC 13 AND SE 1/4 S/E 1/4 SEC 14 AND NW 1/4 NW 1/4 SEC 24 AND NE 1/4 NE /4 SEC23 ALL IN TWP 10
*Orator further states that on the same day, the said Mason executed a bond in the penalty of $600. ...Your Orator further states **the said Mason departed this life on***

or about 20 day of Nov 1853, intestate, leaving him surviving: **Lydia Mason, his** **wife** *(who afterward intermarried with* **James Gosset,** *who has since died. Thomas J Mason,* **Eliza Bays** *the wife of David Bays, the Eliza and her husband have both since died interstate leaving them surviving Alexis Bays and Helen Bays their only children at law:* **Martha Bourland wife of Henry Bourland.** *The Said Martha both since died intestate leaving them surviving* **Franklin Bourland, Samuel Bourland, Harriet Bourland** *who married David Taylor and* **Harvey Bourland***; Alexis Matlby surviving husband and William A Matlby, Martha H Matlby, Christopher C Matlby Cyrus A Matlby surviving children of* **Narcissa Matlby***, deceased daughter of the said Isaac Mason deceased, Harriett Jagers, wife of Thomas Jagers, the said Harriett and her husband both since have died intestate leaving them surviving Elizabeth Sidall wife of John Sidall...* **Robert G Ingersoll** *was granted guardian for all of the above minor heirs....Summonsed: John M Hancock. Hezikiah sought from the Circuit Court of Saline County reimbursement for sheriff and other fees the sum of $24.15 in the June Term of 1858; see B792.*

Just look at the useful findings, generally in bold. From this document I first learned the death date of a grandfather (Isaac Mason), what happened to one of his wives (Lydia Mason Gosset) in another marriage, confirmed the actual first name (Martha) of a grandmother when others thought the grandfather had married a Lydia Mason, the sons of Henry Bourland including the husband of Harriet, and other relationships. A gold mine!

Deeds

Deeds are another useful source. They help define property, reference the past and present owner and can provide some interesting anecdotes through location mapping. This point is better illustrated later in this book under Mapping.

Cemetery Records and Obituaries

Cemetery records are often badly kept, but in some cases much can be learned if the cemetery has been well maintained. Obituaries are a wonderful way to help build out a family, with a daughter's married name and much more. See an example below:

*The Messenger - Thursday, March 9, 2000. Richland, KY. - **William Houston 'Hadicol' Wyatt**, 65, of Richland, **died** at 6:45 p.m. Tuesday March 7, 2000, at Regional Medical Center. He was born in Hopkins Co., Ky., on May 15,1934, to **Myrtle Stills Wyatt Littlepage and the late William Geobel Wyatt**. He was a dragline operator for Peabody Co. River Queen Mines, a member of the UMWA Local #1178, and a member of Richland Missionary Baptist Church. He was a U.S. Army veteran, having served a tour of duty in Korea, a member of the Beulah Masonic Lodge #609 F&AM, a member of Western Kentucky Consistory, and a member of the Rizpah Shrine Temple. He was one of the founders and a trustee of Richland Volunteer Fire Department, a 4H leader, and past president of the 4H Council. He was a charter member of the Western Kentucky Antique Power Association, a Kentucky Colonel, and a member of the Eastern Star #390. He is survived by his **wife of 41 years,** Linda Clayton Wyatt; two sons, **Mark Wyatt and Van Wyatt,** both of Madisonville; **one sister, Jo Ann Hill**, of Mortons Gap, Ky. ; and one granddaughter. Services will be 11a.m. Friday at Barnett - Strother Funeral Home with Bros. Jerry Easley and Pat Cameron officiating. Burial will be in **Silent Run Cemetery.** Visitation will be from 4 until 8 p.m. today at the funeral home. Masonic services will be conducted at 7 p.m. Thursday at the funeral home. Memorial contributions may take the form of donations to Richland Baptist Church. Memorial contribution envelopes will be available at the funeral home.*

Here you learn parental names, approximate date of marriage, church affiliation, activities within the community and children. Another gold mine!

Military Records

Military records can be useful. While a fire in the National Personnel Records Center in St. Louis, MO destroyed many records in 1973, a review of those which survived and those since added may offer interesting material. Many service people may have served in National Guard units in a State and thus State records in turn should be explored.

Other Areas Of Value

And there are other valuable things to locate, listed in the slide below. I would like to highlight City Directories. A year-to-year comparison can often suggest family or person movement from neighborhood to neighborhood, change in occupation and other data of interest. Business records will often name Directors, as will church records for members.

One only has to say to oneself: I want all the data I can find and I will overturn every stone I can. I refer you back to Visiting Your City, County, State; it's all there and some of it will be on the Internet in many cases.

More to look at .....

- Compiled genealogies
- Local Histories - Hopkins 1987
- City Directories
- Maps & Atlases
- Funeral Homes, Cemetery records
- Manuscripts
  - Diaries
  - Church records
  - Business Records

Many people say they have trouble performing research if their parents or grandparents are recent immigrants. Once again Google will suggest many good Sources and provide assistance with that problem.

In addition, England has in 2009 posted a wonderful site at **www.british-history. ac.uk,** plus **www.proni.gov.uk** and **www.Irish-roots.ie** is useful for Northern Ireland. For the French, it's **www.géneanet.com.**

And if foreign country .....

- *Irish Roots: Irish BMD Databases* (74-76) in Family Tree Magazine, May 2008 by Alan Stewart
- *20 Best Sites for Italian Genealogy* (120-41) in Internet Genealogy, May 2008
- *Going Home: a Guide to Polish-American Family History Research* by Jonathan Shea from CCSU
- New Netherland Connections (NY, NJ) Dutch colonial period (1624-1664) dkoenig@LMI.net
- ....or just Google it.......

Chapter Nine

THE NEED FOR ELECTRONIC FOLDERS

You have been collecting many materials from boxes in the attic or basement of others. You should have found useful data on the Internet. Your cousins should have been sending you executed copies of the Family Group Sheets and biographical data.

Some of what you have found, Source documents, will have a label pasted on it with a sequential number and will have been placed in your legal sized manila folders, but after placement into your software.

Other data will be in electronic form and should stay in that form. For example, letters you have typed and sent to cousins, Internet findings and so forth. So there is now a need for electronic folders to enable you to control the filings on your computer and before matters get out of control. You will be greatly surprised at the amount of data you collect.

You will surely need the following:

- Families folder, with an additional Surname folder within for each of the surnames you are researching (and the number here will increase substantially over time);

- Letters folder, for each letter you choose to send in addressee sequence with date; e.g. Barnes, Henry 09/06/12;

- Locations folder, since you will find soon enough that those you are researching live in or have moved to diverse cities, counties, and states and you will have collected information for your Notes; you will need to organize certain data by location;

- Pictures folder, which has been discussed previously and in which you place pictures of relatives using their ID Number from your software;

- Trips folder, to house the Trip Reports, discussed earlier as well.

THE NEED FOR A SURNAME SEARCH LIST

Whenever you e-mail a potential Colleague, whenever you post a query or respond to a query, whenever you write a Colleague – indeed for every communication you initiate - there is a need for a list of the surnames you are researching, as part of your "signature" on the e-mail or letter. And this list will of course get larger over time as you uncover new information.

So you need a paragraph like the following which you can copy/paste into your outgoing correspondence, because you will use it often. It will look like this, in alphabetical order:

I am researching the following surnames and hope you are able to match with some of them so that we might exchange data: Bobbitt, Bourland, Brigham, Cardwell, Flagg, Garfield, King, Mason, etc. etc. Any help you can offer with be gratefully appreciated. I will reciprocate in turn.

To once more insure we are on the right path, let us review the **Work Plan** steps that have been identified since Chapter 5:

- Visit Cities, Counties, Libraries, History & Genealogical Societies

- Write Trip Reports

- Locate "mugbooks"

- Use your software, starting with you and your family

- Prepare for Final Report, your Legacy

- Research and capture data from Census, Birth, Death, Deeds, etc.

- Get blank copy of all Census forms

- Prepare electronic folders; Families, Letters, Locations, Pictures, Trips

- Prepare surname search list for all communications

Chapter Ten

ADVANCED TOPICS

We will next cover some advanced topics. Some of the following discussions or suggestions are not for everyone. Many of the tasks can be performed later after you have a good start on your Goals. But you should be aware of them nonetheless, and try as many as you can or wish to.

GEDCOMs

First, a discussion of GEDCOMs. GEDCOM is an acronym for Genealogical Data Communications. A GEDCOM is essentially a computer program which almost all genealogical software systems incorporate and that allows the electronic exchange of data between diverse hardware and software systems.

Advanced Topics

- Guidance
  - GEDCOMs
  - Browse
  - DNA studies
  - Miscellaneous
- Hire professional
- Mapping
- Printing

Thus, a user of Reunion on the Macintosh could exchange data with a Family Tree Maker user on an IBM or Dell PC.

There are different versions of GEDCOMs and as a consequence some data from System 1 may not make it to System 2, but generally it is a convenient way to send data to a Colleague for use on her system.

On the next page is an example of a GEDCOM file. You may get one, double click to open it and wonder - what in the world is this?

What you are looking at on the next page is a small sample of a GEDCOM. This one is Version 5.5 used as part of Leister Productions' Reunion software system.

```
0 HEAD
1 SOUR Reunion
2 VERS V8.0
2 CORP Leister Productions
1 DEST Reunion
1 DATE 11 FEB 2006
1 FILE test
1 GEDC
2 VERS 5.5
1 CHAR MACINTOSH
0 @I1@ INDI
1 NAME Bob /Cox/
1 SEX M
1 FAMS @F1@
1 CHAN
2 DATE 11 FEB 2006
0 @I2@ INDI
1 NAME Joann /Para/
1 SEX F
1 FAMS @F1@
1 CHAN
2 DATE 11 FEB 2006
0 @I3@ INDI
1 NAME Bobby Jo /Cox/
1 SEX M
1 FAMC @F1@
1 CHAN
2 DATE 11 FEB 2006
0 @F1@ FAM
1 HUSB @I1@
1 WIFE @I2@
1 MARR
1 CHIL @I3@
0 TRLR
```

It covers a family named Cox, whose husband is Bob, wife named Joann Para (Cox) and a son named Bobby Jo. You know they belong to one family because the Family code – F1 – is used with all three people.

This particular example does not have a Note, a birth and death and so forth but that data, if available, comes across the two systems as well.

Lastly, the first line is "0 Head", standing for Header, and the last line is "0 TRLR" standing for Trailer.

You need not worry about any of this beyond recognizing which attachments to an e-mail are GEDCOMs.

You need to decide as mentioned earlier whether you will import a GEDCOM directly into your database. My choice was not to import directly. Here is what I do. I open my software and say that I want a New family file. I import the GEDCOM into the New file and then run a Register Report. From there I decide which data is "in my style' and which is not. Usually it is not in my style, since it comes with many abbreviations, punctuation in names, indented paragraphs and so forth.

So I then type that data I wish to use fresh to my system or Copy and Paste with manual corrections.

You are obviously free to set your own standards, but I would strongly suggest you set some standards and stick by them for the sake of consistency.

GUIDANCE - BROWSE CERTAIN WEB SITES

There are many Internet sites you should at least browse to see if there are data there in which you would be interested.

You should consider joining a DNA surname group with your name, if one exists. There are several places that perform DNA tests. One is listed below and is **www. familytreeDNA.com**.

Guidance - www.familytreeDNA.com.

The DNA test is completely painless and involves no more than swabbing the inside of your mouth, placing the swab in a supplied packet and mailing it off to the testing facility. Your DNA values will then be compared to others with your name if you are male since those values are passed father to son to son and on down. These are called yDNA.

Guidance - Browse

- Join applicable DNA Groups
  - yDNA   - (fathers to sons)
  - mtDNA   - Mitochondrial (female to children)
  - http://www.familytreeDNA.com/surname.aspx
- Consider or join myfamily groups
- Join family associations
- Go to county, city, state web sites

The female mtDNA or mitochondrial is passed from mothers to all children. There is less experience as of this writing with the mtDNA and I will leave it to familytreeDNA or others to explain the expectations one should have.

I do have experience with yDNA. We joined a large group of Bollings, we being Bourlands, because some thought we might be related. So far we are not, but the tests allow separation by spelling and test results and here are some of the important results we Bourlands have experienced.

There are 12 marker, 25, 37 and 67 marker tests available with our vendor; each more expensive than the other. I have found the 12 marker useless and would recommend no less than 37, with 67 preferable.

My extended family has had 21 tested persons and found that those we know who are serious genealogists can use a DNA proof of their descent and relationship. There have been several who fall completely out of the descent. This would be caused by faulty research, ancestors who have changed their names, adopted individuals or other errors.

The most interesting test was performed on a Bowland family whom our Bourland Society had claimed quite vociferously were Bourland clan members and we absolutely knew for some 25 years where they belonged in the tree. One of them constantly for those same 25 years maintained that we were, well, crazy. I convinced her to get her brother to take the yDNA test, and she was correct! DNA said they were not Bourlands. That was the end of that discussion.

Guidance - MyFamily Groups

Another useful Ancestry.com site is **www.myFamily.com**. This is an Internet site which allows someone to set up a site dedicated to a particular family surname, offers others an opportunity to join and thus manage a small group of like-minded researchers to share and exchange data on a family. This is particularly useful for new researchers as they may find numerous Colleagues interested in the same surname on their way to the Goal of 2-300 as set earlier. It is a way of quickly alerting and sharing with others newly found information.

You should go to the site and see if there is a group and ask if you can join them. Else, create one for your own surname.

Guidance - Family Associations

There are many family organizations, many of which have a web site. There is no normal naming convention for these sites, so you must look hard using Google, Clusty or another search engine. One such organization is the edmund-rice.org, which has an obscure URL which will give you an idea of the difficulties you will face. But if you can spend some time using a variety of search criteria, what you do find will provide you with much information.

Guidance - City, County and State Web Sites

This had been discussed before but much emphasis is required because most cities, counties and states have excellent web site with considerable data. Look at **www.kykinfolk.com/hopkins/** as an example of an excellent county site.

HIRE A PROFESSIONAL GENEALOGIST

It may be useful to spend money to hire a professional genealogist for your "brick walls," for example, a grandmother you simply can not locate data about. Certainly it can help you decide that your efforts have not been useless if those who research for a career are unable to help as well. If they do find data for you, it's another serendipity.

I got together with a cousin to split the admittedly smallish funds required to hire several professionals to help get us back from 1654 in Maryland to the White family who sent the immigrant from England. The first one was from Johns Hopkins - he found nothing. The second was a well-respected author and researcher named Robert W. Barnes who has written many books on Maryland families. We asked him to look through all of his works for help on our family. He too was unable to offer useful data. We then hired an English researcher and he provided us with numerous pages resulting from his study of the family, annotating the many White families at which he had looked. When we asked him how much further would he suggest we keep going after the first effort, he told us, with a touch of humor, that we could not possibly have enough money to look as far as we needed with such a common name! So we were not successful. But some people who have taken my class have had good luck and benefited from their expenditures. But be careful here with open ended searches. Restrict and announce the amount you are willing to spend.

In order to be safe you should hire a person who is a member of the Association of Professional Genealogists (APG) or who has been certified by the Board for Certification of Genealogists (BCG). Both sign a code of ethics and offer mediation services for disputes. Go to **www.apgen.org** and **www.bcgcertification.org**.

CONSIDER MAPPING SOFTWARE

Many genealogists become interested in mapping the various plots of land, whether a Patent provided by royalty or a Headright provided by a government for bringing passengers to this country during its infancy, or a Land Grant the United States gave to those who fought in our early wars or even land bought from another person.

I direct your attention to **www.DirectLineSoftware.com** which sells mapping software and, as part of their sales program on the web site lists others who use the software by State, County and City. Were you to explore this possibility, you may find your equivalent to my serendipity. Below is a map reflecting early Henrico County, VA patents which Thomas T. Bannister, in 2002 a professor at the University of Rochester, posted on the Internet. Mr. Bannister's Internet address was: rochester. edu/college/BIO/bannister/. At that address is a work entitled in part, Mapping 17th Century Patents on the North Side of the James River, between Varina and World's End in Henrico County.

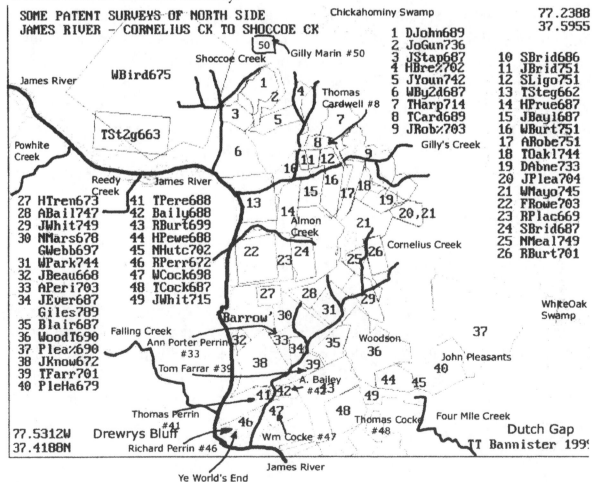

I took his work and added a darker color to the James River and associated creeks. I added the full name of the owner with an arrow to his/her property. Property #6 is the approximate center of modern day downtown Richmond, VA. If you look at #8 and then go to the 8th number, you see TCARD689. This interprets to: Thomas Cardwell obtained this land near Gilly's Creek in 1689.

Now if you go to #41 and #46, Thomas Perrin in 1688 and Richard Perrin in 1672, you would guess they are brothers, one of whom named his property Ye World's End, the 'Ye' old style for 'The'.

I have previously referred to the possibility of building a novel out of some facts. Here we go. Thomas Cardwell (1686-1772) was my 6th Great Grandfather and he married Martha Perrin (1688- ?) in the Varina Parish about 1711. I have Sources for that data.

So, now I quote from my book on the Cardwells:

"It would have been natural for young Thomas Cardwell to either ride his horse across the fields and streams to court Martha, else to get into his canoe and float down Gilly's Creek to the James River and then paddle to Ye World's End in time for dinner, or "suppa" as they say in Richmond, and courting the beautiful Martha. Neither could have taken more than an hour's effort as they were but an approximate 3 miles apart."

THOUGHTS ON PRINTING, PUBLISHING

The ultimate result from your Goal of writing a book requires some thinking on your part. The cost of hard bound books today is relatively inexpensive because the world of computers has given rise to PODs, or companies who "print on demand" from one to hundreds of copies as you request.

In 2009 the cost of a hardbound book, black and white, with 130 pages would cost about $1,700. A paperback of that same book on publisher grade paper, black and white, 8½ x 11" and perfect-bound, would cost $479 at Lulu.com. Prices of course are estimates.

I did not wish to spend that much for the other books I wanted to publish. So for them, I composed them as discussed earlier and printed them as a Portable

Document Format (.pdf) file. I then burned a CD on my own computer, attached a CD cover using a Memorex CD Labeler appropriately designed and I was finished, all of this "printing" (a CD) costing next to nothing extra.

Here my advantages included color, which costs a great deal on paper, and the fact that my books were now electronically searchable. Of great importance, the document can be read by the free Adobe Reader. And since younger children today read less and less unless it's on the computer, a substantial potential increase in readership.

Since a grandmother might well lead to a dozen surnames to whom you are related (they being great grandparents, great uncles and the like) the use of PDF allows you to have chapters on each of those surnames. You can either buy Adobe Professional for about $500 or go to Federal Express/Kinkos, and for a small fee for the use of that software, have them make Chapters out of your Register Reports for each surname using that software.

In addition, if there are special parts of your work you wish to highlight in the Index, maybe a map or picture or special write-up, Adobe Professional can highlight that for you and make the entire effort that much more rewarding.

If you wish to know more about printing, go to **www.Parapub.com**. If you wish to see a front cover of a "pdf" book, with Chapters and special sections, see Appendix 2.

LEGAL AND PROPERTY TERMS

Let me cover a few terms you will face in your research; others can be found using Google or another search engine.

Legal Terms:

Guardian ad litem	Guardian for children assigned by Court
Intestate	No will at death
Nuncupative will	Oral will
Teste	Witness
Testate	Valid will

Property Terms:

Headright	50 acres/immigrant passage paid
Moity	One half
Messuage	Home and outer buildings, land
Patent	Government to owner

PRESERVING YOUR TREASURES

Many of the items found in your research should be preserved for posterity. It may be your parents' marriage certificate, or special letters your parents wrote, photos, bedspreads, family Bibles, even tools or jewelry. Each and every one of us will have different criteria for what should be preserved. When you do preserve, be sure to follow these rules:

- Use acid free materials, no plastic

- Test clothe for colorfastness

- Store in polyester film: Mylar D or Melinex 516

- Hydrate and flatten carefully

- Use Archival Mist or encapsulate

There are certain guidelines that apply. Use acid free materials and never use plastic. Excellent materials are available from Light Impressions and others and include ultraclear sealable bags in various sizes. Or the same item in a long roll that can be cut to fit. Go to **www.lightimpressions.com** among other sites.

Old documents are often rolled or folded and stuck in chests and drawers before someone decides they are worth preserving. They have aged in their shape and can break with handling. They are dry and require hydrating. Go to

http://www.iigs.org/newsletter/9906news/olddocs.htm.en

and follow the instructions. There are numerous places one can go to obtain professional advice on preservation matters. Here are some examples:

- General Information – **www.GeorgiaArchives.org** or **www.sos.georgia.gov/archives**
- Preserving Books - **www.nedcc.org**
- Photo Preservation - **www.lightimpressions.com**
- Conservator - American Institute of Conservators **www.alc.org**

You will find equivalent organizations in many states and large cities and, again, the use of Google can help you identify them.

HOW TO WRITE AN AUTOBIOGRAPHY

I have earlier said I believe it is nearly criminal for you not to write an autobiography to leave for your children and grandchildren. Here are some thoughts in that regard.

Decide why you are writing your autobiography. Is it to be published, kept private for your descendants, or other? I have been writing mine for over ten years. It's about 70 pages long at this point with pictures. It is not a picture book, but shows and discusses places my children have never

How To Write an Autobiography

- Understand why you are writing
- Read other people's
- Think about your audience, your theme
- Organize (chronological is popular)
- Jog your memory - photos, letters, etc,
- Use descriptive, vivid, interesting words
- Edit ..... and preserve it safely
- Start writing

(you owe it to your world)

seen, such as my homes in the 25 years before their births. It includes my early activities, summer camps, schools, noteworthy friends, humorous adventures and just plain adventures. I add to it every once in a while as I remember events from the past. No one has ever read it and probably no one will until I am gone. Your approach will most likely be different. But give it thought. Your children and especially your grandchildren will be glad you did, just as you would be if your parents and grandparents had done so.

Chapter Eleven

FINAL THOUGHTS BEFORE REVIEW

As I have said before, I hope your Goal is for you to write a book. There are many ways to approach that task. Pick a family, a person and start writing a biography or a novel built around your genealogy. Or, use the Register Report capability of your software to create one. Below is one page from what could be called a book, a Register Report from the genealogy software:

First Generation

1. Charles Rice Cardwell, G Grandfather. Born on 28 Jul 1852 in Manitou, Hopkins Cty, KY. Charles Rice died in Alms House, Springfield, Greene Cty, MO, on 5 May 1927; he was 74. Charles Rice was buried in Hazelwood Cemetery, Springfield, Greene Cty, MO. Occupation: Farmer, Gambler, Saloonkeeper, Real estate.

On 15 Mar 1876 when Charles Rice was 23, he first married Emily Clay Graham, G Grandmother, daughter of Col Harvey Graham & Mary Ann Baker, in Col Graham's Home, Madisonville, Hopkins Cty, KY. Born on 30 Jul 1852 in Madisonville, Hopkins Cty, KY. Emily Clay died in Madisonville, Hopkins Cty, KY, in 1879; she was 26. Emily Clay was buried in White School House Cemetery, Madisonville, Hopkins Cty, KY.

They had the following children:
2	i.	Mary Elizabeth Cardwell (1877-1963)
3	ii.	Thomas K Cardwell (~1878-1879)

On 25 Mar 1880 when Charles Rice was 27, he second married Fannie E Baker, 1C3R, daughter of William Richard Baker & Mary M Whitfield, in The William Baker Home, Madisonville, Hopkins Cty, KY. Born on 16 Feb 1860 in Madisonville, Hopkins Cty, KY. Fannie E died in Parr's Rest Home, Louisville, Jefferson Cty, KY, on 30 Jan 1936; she was 75.

All the preceding Register page required was a Name, Birth, Death, Marriage and Burial date and location and occupations. The page required a husband and his wife and their children with that same data. ALL THE REST WAS WRITTEN

BY MY SOFTWARE. Call it a Reportwriter.

Let me take one family from the above Register and show what the computer wrote for me, in italics:

First Generation

---

1. Charles Rice Cardwell, *G Grandfather. Born on* 28 Jul 1852 *in* Manitou, Hopkins Cty, KY. *Charles Rice died in* Alms House, Springfield, Greene Cty, MO, *on* 5 May 1927; *he was 74. Charles Rice was buried in* Hazelwood Cemetery, Springfield, Greene Cty, MO. *Occupation:* Farmer, Gambler, Saloonkeeper, Real estate.

On 15 Mar 1876 *when Charles Rice was 23, he first married* Emily Clay Graham, *GGrandmother, daughter of* Col Harvey Graham & Mary Ann Baker, *in* Col Graham's Home, Madisonville, Hopkins Cty, KY. *Born on* 30 Jul 1852 *in* Madisonville, Hopkins Cty, KY. Emily Clay *died in* Madisonville, Hopkins Cty, KY, *in* 1879; *she was 26.* Emily Clay *was buried in* White School House Cemetery, Madisonville, Hopkins Cty, KY.

They had the following children:
    2   i.   *Mary Elizabeth Cardwell (1877-1963)*
    3   ii.   *Thomas K Cardwell (~1878-1879)*

On 25 Mar 1880 *when Charles Rice was 27, he second married* Fannie E Baker, *1C3R, daughter of William Richard Baker & Mary M Whitfield, in* The William Baker Home, Madisonville, Hopkins Cty, KY. *Born on 16 Feb 1860 in* Madisonville, Hopkins Cty, KY. *Fannie E died in* Parr's Rest Home, Louisville, Jefferson Cty, KY, *on* 30 Jan 1936; *she was 75.*

So you see, the basic writing is performed largely by the software; you have only added Name, Birth, Death, Marriage and Burial date and Location as well as Occupations.

However, there should be more - as such a book would be boring with just dates and places. So you must add Notes, which would be biographical data sent to you by your cousins; information found in newspapers, the Internet, books pertaining to the person; information on the time, the location, whatever information you can locate and determine is of interest.

I would guess I have personally typed about 10-20% of my Notes out of some 3,000 pages. Not as much effort as you would have guessed!!

By the way, in all examples of a Register or Ahnentafel Report in this book I have not provided the Sources only to reduce the size of the representation. Trust me, there are Sources available as I have emphasized repeatedly.

And thus I will end with final guidance, just before a review;

My Major Guidance

- Document your sources
- Work on the distaff side of your lines
- Be Aggressive: email, telephone, visits
- Write your autobiography; convince others to do so
- Write a "book", it's easier than it looks with Internet, Other people, Auto-fill in, Reportwriter, Copy/Paste

The next chapter reviews the Work Plan this book has presented to help you arrive at your Goal, whether that Goal is to write a book or books, document your family or whatever Goal you have selected.

I conclude as I began, with hope that your genealogy journey will be as meaningful and fun for you as mine has been for me.

You are destined to uncover wild characters, poignant stories, little-known vignettes, and surprising revelations. You will "meet" your ancestors and find them wonderful, brilliant, eccentric, crazy, and unique, and they will make you laugh and they may make you cry. You will gain new understanding, and perhaps even greater respect, for those you know well, and those recently found. You will answer some questions and you will accept that some questions may never be answered.

And you will grow from the experience. You only have one family; each of those who appear in your lineage is, in some large or small way, part of who you are. Embrace the findings and marvel at the revelations.

And then pass them on.

Create your legacy not only for yourself, but also for the generations who follow. Your children and their children will be as curious about you as you were about your ancestors. Give your descendants the benefit of your research and the wisdom of your insights.

And enjoy every minute of the ride.

Chapter Twelve

AND NOW A BRIEF REVIEW OF OUR COMPLETE WORK PLAN

(1) Buy and learn to use a computer and software

(2) Buy legal sized manila folders and a box of labels

(3) Buy Everton's *Handybook for Genealogists*

(4) Get to know your Software; Use it on your family

(5) Record Source documents in your Software or a Spreadsheet

(6) Join ancestry.com & NEHGS & Familysearch.com & CyndisList.

(7) Work from the known to the unknown

(8) Work with a wide focus

(9) Send Family Group Sheets (FGS or FGR) to all known relatives and ask for biographies and names and addresses of cousins they know

(10) Review photos: go to photodetective.com (Maureen Taylor)

(11) Interview all older, some younger, relatives – tape, type

(12) Determine what is in "siblings' attic"

(13) Start a Pedigree Chart

(14) Learn and use worldconnect.genealogy.rootsweb.com or gencircles.com

(15) Search for your surnames, enroll in Surname & County Lists
- Go to rootsweb.com
- On Home page go to Mailing Lists
  - Then go to Index
    Enroll in your Surnames and Counties
- Go to archiver.rootsweb.com/th/index/SURNAME (Yours)

(16) Document your Sources–Elizabeth Mills, *Evidence, Citation & Analysis*

(17) Do a Google search on all of your surnames

(18) Organize your data

(19) Visit city/county/state; historical and genealogical societies in your counties: http://www.rootsweb.com/~kyhopkin (tilde and 2 for state+6 for county) or Google

(20) Search "mugbooks" at turnerpublishing.com

(21) Write Trip reports for city, county, state visits

(22) Allen County, PL, BYU, Latter Day Saints, Ladson, NEHGS

(23) Get copy of all Census forms – 1790 to 1930

(24) Join family associations – Google search for address

(25) Look at:
   - Census records

- Birth, death records
- Marriage certificates
- Wills, Probate records
- Deeds, patents, grants
- Cemetery records
- Obituaries
- Court records
- Funeral homes
- Military and church records
- City directories

(26) Prepare for your Legacy, your book

(27) Prepare electronic folders: Families, Letters, Locations, Pictures, Trips

(28) Prepare surname search list

(29) For publishing your book, go to parapub.com or lulu.com

(30) For publishing your book: Use Acrobat Professional for book Chapter (surnames) at Kinkos and Memorex CD Labeler for CD cover

(31) Best research example: www.freepages.genealogy.rootsweb.com/~berry/

(32) Go to every Internet Address on Appendix 3.

(33) Start your autobiography; get spouse started

(34) Work hard on the distaff or female side of your heritage

(35) Reach a Goal of 2-300 Colleagues

(36) Preserve your treasures

Appendix 1
TRADEMARK Acknowledgements

Ancestry.com
360 W. 4800 N
Provo, UT 84604
owns the following trademarks:

Ancestry.com; Myfamily.com; Genealogy.com; Rootsweb.com; TGN.com;
FamilyTreeMaker.com; Family Tree Maker software

Rootsmagic, Inc.
P.O. Box 495
Springville, UT 84663
owns the Rootsmagic software trademark.

The Church of Jesus Christ of Latter Day Saints
3751 South 2200 West
Salt Lake City UT 84119
owns the Personal Ancestral File software trademark.

Wholly Genes Software
9110 Red Branch Road Suite O
Columbia MD 21045
owns the Master Genealogist software trademark.

Millennia Corporation
P.O. Box 9410
Surprise AZ 85374
owns the Legacy Family Tree software trademark.

Leister Productions, Inc.
P.O. Box 289
Mechanicsburg PA 17055
owns the Reunion software trademark.

Apple, Inc.
Cupertino CA 95014
owns the Macintosh trademark.

Appendix 2
Sample Front Page of a ".PDF" Book

Below is a picture of the front page of a book being read by Adobe Reader. The book itself was comprised of Chapters using Register Reports from the genealogical software for the various surnames, such as Baer, Baker, etc. It was then compiled into a book by Adobe Acrobat Professional, while at the same time adding Bookmarks for the various Chapters and other highlights such as Recollections and Roland Brothers.

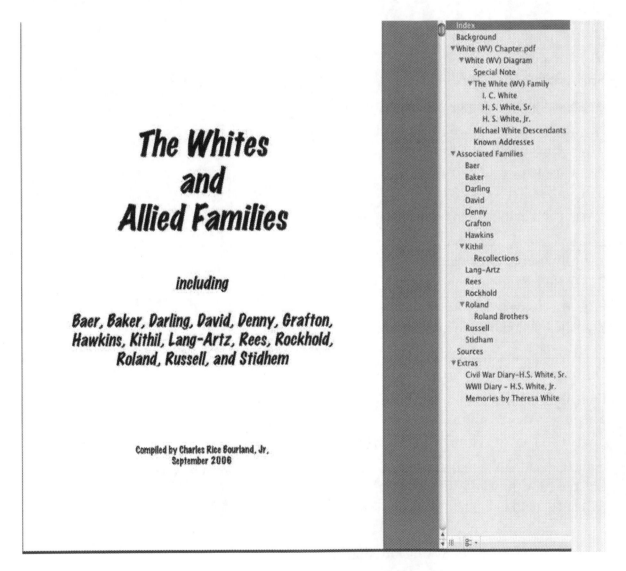

Adobe Reader and Adobe Acrobat Professional are trademarks of Adobe Systems, Inc.

Appendix 3
Internet Addresses

ANCESTRY.COM
>   Ancestry.com
BERRY   (Example of best research)
>   http://freepages.genealogy.rootsweb.com/~berry/
COUNTY, SURNAME ASSOCIATIONS
>   rootsweb.ancestry.com/~kyhopkin tildé, 2 char state, 6 for county
DNA
>   familytreeDNA.com/surname.aspx
DUTCH COLONIAL, NY, NJ
>   newenglandancestors.org/database_search/NewNetherlandConnections.
>   asp
ELLIS ISLAND
>   EllisIsland.org
EUROPE
>   british-history.ac.uk; proni.gov.uk; irish-roots.ie; geneanet.com
ILLINOIS   (example of state offerings)
>   cyberdriveillinois.com
JESUS CHRIST OF THE LATTER DAY SAINTS
>   familysearch.com
LIBRARIES
>   www.acpl..lib.in.us ; lib.byu.edu   ; immigrants.byu.edu   ; script.byu.
MAPPING
>   DirectLineSoftware.com
MUGBOOKS
>   Turnerpublishing.com ; higginsonbooks.com ; newberry.org
myFAMILY
>   myfamily.com
NEHGS
>   NewEnglandAncestors.org
PRESERVATION; HYDRATING
>   Lightimpressionsdirect.com; www.iigs.org/newsletter/9906news/olddocs.
>   htm.en
PUBLISHING
>   ParaPublishing.com ; LuLu.com   ; CafePress.com

Appendix 3
Internet Addresses, continued

SURNAME ASSOCIATIONS   (an example, use Google)
　　　edmund-rice.org
WORLD CONNECT
　　　wc.rootsweb.ancestry.com
WORTH
　　　measuringworth.com

Family Group Sheet

Husband's full name _____

    Born _____ Place of birth _____

    Married _____ Place of marriage _____

    Died _____ Place of death _____

    Buried _____ Place of burial _____

    Name of husband's father _____

    Name of husband's mother (use maiden name) _____

    Names of other wives _____

Wife's full name _____

    Born _____ Place of birth _____

    Married _____ Place of marriage _____

    Died _____ Place of death _____

    Buried _____ Place of burial _____

    Name of wife's father _____

    Name of wife's mother (use maiden name) _____

    Names of other husbands _____

1. Child's full name _____ Full name of spouse _____

    Born _____ Place of birth _____

    Married _____ Place of marriage _____

    Died _____ Place of death _____

    Buried _____ Place of burial _____

2. Child's full name _____ Full name of spouse _____

    Born _____ Place of birth _____

    Married _____ Place of marriage _____

    Died _____ Place of death _____

    Buried _____ Place of burial _____

3. Child's full name _____ Full name of spouse _____

    Born _____ Place of birth _____

    Married _____ Place of marriage _____

    Died _____ Place of death _____

    Buried _____ Place of burial _____

4. Child's full name _____ Full name of spouse _____

    Born _____ Place of birth _____

    Married _____ Place of marriage _____

    Died _____ Place of death _____

    Buried _____ Place of burial _____

5. Child's full name _____ Full name of spouse _____

    Born _____ Place of birth _____

    Married _____ Place of marriage _____

    Died _____ Place of death _____

    Buried _____ Place of burial _____

Notes _____

_____

NEW ENGLAND HISTORIC GENEALOGICAL SOCIETY®
www.NewEnglandAncestors.org

© NEHGS 2003

Appendix 5

Pedigree Chart

Chart # _____

Number 1 on this chart is the same as
number _____ on chart number _____.

*Use the spaces to the right to enter the chart
numbers on which the lines continue.*

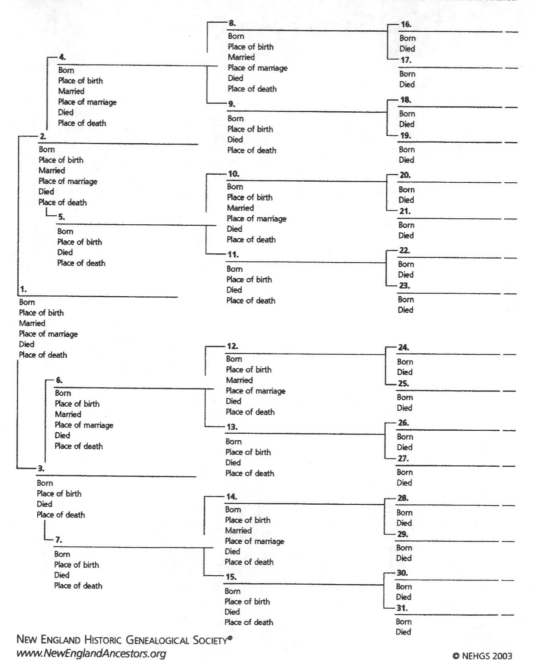

8.
Born
Place of birth
Married
Place of marriage
Died
Place of death

16.
Born
Died

17.
Born
Died

4.
Born
Place of birth
Married
Place of marriage
Died
Place of death

9.
Born
Place of birth
Died
Place of death

18.
Born
Died

19.
Born
Died

2.
Born
Place of birth
Married
Place of marriage
Died
Place of death

10.
Born
Place of birth
Married
Place of marriage
Died
Place of death

20.
Born
Died

21.
Born
Died

5.
Born
Place of birth
Died
Place of death

11.
Born
Place of birth
Died
Place of death

22.
Born
Died

23.
Born
Died

1.
Born
Place of birth
Married
Place of marriage
Died
Place of death

12.
Born
Place of birth
Married
Place of marriage
Died
Place of death

24.
Born
Died

25.
Born
Died

6.
Born
Place of birth
Married
Place of marriage
Died
Place of death

13.
Born
Place of birth
Died
Place of death

26.
Born
Died

27.
Born
Died

3.
Born
Place of birth
Died
Place of death

14.
Born
Place of birth
Married
Place of marriage
Died
Place of death

28.
Born
Died

29.
Born
Died

7.
Born
Place of birth
Died
Place of death

15.
Born
Place of birth
Died
Place of death

30.
Born
Died

31.
Born
Died

NEW ENGLAND HISTORIC GENEALOGICAL SOCIETY®
www.NewEnglandAncestors.org

© NEHGS 2003